# The Theology of Suffering and Death

This book offers a theological foundation for engaging with the realities of suffering and dying. Designed particularly for practical theology students and trainee caregivers, it introduces the spiritual and theological issues raised by suffering and dying. The chapters consider:

- how Christian theology deals with the problem of suffering and how the Bible treats these difficult issues;
- post-Biblical interpretations of Jesus' suffering and the Cross;
- modern instances including ecology, poverty, discrimination, and war;
- comparative religious approaches and depiction in popular culture.

Natalie Kertes Weaver relates theology to practical issues of caregiving and provides a "toolbox" for thinking about suffering and death in a creative and supportive way.

**Natalie Kertes Weaver** is Associate Professor of Religious Studies at Ursuline College in Ohio, USA. Her books include *Marriage and Family: A Christian Theological Foundation* (2009) and *Christian Thought and Practice: A Primer* (2012).

# The Theology of Suffering and Death

## An Introduction for Caregivers

Natalie Kertes Weaver

Routledge
Taylor & Francis Group
LONDON AND NEW YORK

First published 2013
by Routledge
2 Park Square, Milton Park, Abingdon, Oxon OX14 4RN

Simultaneously published in the USA and Canada by Routledge
711 Third Avenue, New York, NY 10017

*Routledge is an imprint of the Taylor & Francis Group, an informa business*



*British Library Cataloguing in Publication Data*
A catalogue record for this book is available from the British Library

*Library of Congress Cataloging in Publication Data*
Kertes Weaver, Natalie.
The theology of suffering and death : an introduction for caregivers / Natalie Kertes Weaver.
p. cm.
Includes index.
1. Suffering--Religious aspects--Christianity. 2. Death--Religious aspects--Christianity. 3. Caring--Religious aspects--Christianity. I. Title.
BV4909.K47 2013
231'.8--dc23
2012033969

ISBN: 978-0-415-78107-7 (hbk)
ISBN: 978-0-415-78108-4 (pbk)
ISBN: 978-0-203-07992-8 (ebk)

Typeset in Sabon
by Taylor & Francis Books

Printed and bound in Great Britain by the MPG Books Group

For my sister, Elissa

# Contents

# Acknowledgments

When I began teaching, I felt inadequate to speak about suffering because every person is ultimately called to endure his or her own circumstances in a uniquely personal way. It was (and continues to be) a challenge to find the right balance between theological content, personal example, and professional experience. In the end, study of suffering is not so much about knowing and teaching content as it is about learning through the compassionate witness we bear to our own lives and to the journeys of one another. That witness can be meaningfully studied and evaluated, but it meets real success only when the whole classroom brings an openness, transparency, and authenticity to the task. I am deeply grateful for all of the students of Ursuline College with whom I have had the privilege to study and learn. This book represents foremost the generosity of spirit and wisdom of those classrooms.

In addition, I have been personally inspired by the example of courage and dignity in the face of loss or struggle of a number of family members and friends, whose lessons and experiences are never far from my mind:

- For those who survived the deaths of children, including especially the families of Raymond Lawrence and Jacob Weber;
- In memory of the elder deaths in my family, including especially Margret Kertes and Bertha Lawrence;
- For my courageous friends, including especially the Shields and Maxel families.

I would finally like to acknowledge:

- My mother, husband and sons, for edifying conversation;
- The wonderful writers and authors referenced in my book, from whose experience and knowledge I have learned copiously;
- Cleveland's Catholic Community Connection Abundant Life team, especially Pam Maidens and Antoinette Horn;
- The editorial staff at Routledge, who have graciously developed this book with me;
- My former teachers at Pepperdine University, from whom I learned my foremost goal as an educator, "Freely ye received, freely give." (Matthew 10:8)

# Introduction

> When I surveyed all that my hands had done and what I toiled to achieve, everything was meaningless, a chasing after wind; nothing was gained under the sun.
>
> Ecclesiastes 2:11

One day in my class on the theology of suffering, my student tells a story. Some relatives were visiting for her twenty-first birthday, and everyone was going to dinner for a celebration. They would not all fit in one car, so she and her mother decided to drive separately. The larger group left first in the van, and she and her mother were grateful for a few minutes to get ready alone. As she was fixing her hair, however, she became aware of a strange gurgling sound coming from down the hall, followed by a loud thud. She was terrified to move. When she eventually did go down the hall into her mother's room, she found her mother supine, foaming at the mouth, eyes rolling back, her body rigid. My student forgot everything she had learned as a nurse-in-training. Time stood still as she waited for emergency medical services to arrive. Her mother remained in a coma for several days. Although her mother survived, my student was deeply scarred by the event. In class, she asks me whether I think God is punishing her for being disrespectful to her mother over the past few years. She mentions learning in church that God punishes children who do not honor their mother and father.

Another student shares that she lost a child. She and her husband then divorced because he told her why it had happened. He said it was his fault. He had been faithless and God was punishing him by taking his child's life. He tells her God also punished King David's child with death because of David's sin with Bathsheba. My student is now multiply devastated: the death; the faithlessness; the divorce; God.

A non-traditional aged student is in my class on the theology of suffering. We watch a video about Thea Bowman's battle with bone cancer. After the video, she shares that she is fighting cancer. I now recall that she has spoken about her teenage child in nearly every class session. In that same class, another student sends me an email late one night asking what happens to people who do not believe. Do they go to Hell? Do they simply wink out of existence? Her friend has committed suicide so she wonders what has happened to his soul. "Could there be multiple possible outcomes depending on a person's beliefs?" she asks. She has no answers, but she cannot avoid the question.

Since I have been teaching the theology of suffering, I have watched students lose parents, siblings, grandparents, and lovers. Their beloveds have passed from childhood illnesses, cancer, heart disease, murder, war, and even work-related death. One student's brother was badly burned in a household fire. These issues all compound other types of issues they are facing: job loss, encroaching poverty, and divorce alongside the more regular challenges of parenting, appliance failures, car accidents, and even household floods. Some of my students are veterans. All of them are aware of violence and injustice in their midst – beginning in their neighborhoods and extending throughout the world community.

Most of the students I encounter are nurses-in-training, and many have enrolled in my theology class because they need it as a requirement for their liberal arts degree. They picked "theology of suffering" because it seemed more relevant than some other courses they could have taken, but after a few weeks of study they are hooked. They have learned that theology is about "faith seeking understanding," and now they genuinely want to understand. Why *did* my mom get sick? What is going to happen to my friend *who committed suicide*? *Why* is the world so violent? These students bring their searching questions to the classroom not because I am their counselor, or their psychologist, or their pastor. They share these questions because I am their theology teacher, and they rightly intuit that theology might provide some answers.

Their questions are ultimately about the origins, purpose, and destiny of human life. They center on the meaning of life, especially insofar as meaning seems to be challenged by their experiences of pain and loss. Their nascent theological questioning illustrates what has become a perennial and profound insight of my teaching and research: nothing engages the theological imagination more than the experience of human pain and suffering.

As I have attempted to address my student concerns over the years, I have used many types of materials and approaches. In that process, I have attempted to find the right blend of theological sources, clinical experiences, and caregiving tools to speak philosophically, practically, and comprehensively to the range of issues that suffering surfaces. This text represents the insights of a decade of teaching and studying the theology of suffering with people who are training for careers in the helping professions (particularly nurses, social workers, ministers, and psychologists). I have adopted an approach that attends to the experience of suffering as an essential frame for Christian theological dialogue, complemented by a practical discussion of spiritual pain and its pastoral care.

Chapter One provides an introductory discussion of the problem of theodicy, considering some classic responses to the theological challenge of suffering. Chapters Two and Three respectively discuss the issue of suffering in the Hebrew and

Christian texts of the Bible. Chapters Four and Five explore in developmental perspective the theological category of soteriology and Christian interpretations of the meaning of Jesus' suffering from the post-biblical through the contemporary periods. Chapter Six undertakes a discussion of suffering in comparative religious perspective through a consideration of suffering in Judaism, Islam, Hinduism, Buddhism, and Daoism. Chapter Seven investigates spiritual and religious issues that arise in the context of suffering, looking at both common spiritual issues as well as special considerations that arise under intensely challenging circumstances. Chapter Eight presents tools for thinking about death and its theological significance. It discusses classical exercises, such as those described by Christian contemplatives and mystics, as well as tools gleaned from the modern hospice movement – including journaling, writing a life's review, completing a spiritual inventory, and music and art therapies.

I anticipate this book's principal application as a primary textbook in a course dealing with theology, suffering, and helping professions. While the text is attentive to a professional caregiver's perspective, it is intended to explore a wide breadth of themes accessible to all persons interested in the theoretical and applied questions and intersections between faith, suffering, and dying. In such a course, the textbook will helpfully be paired with primary source readings from the Bible, the theological tradition, clinical research articles, interviews, and so on. The text will also be useful for persons interested in theology of suffering who cannot devote a full semester to its study. Directors and participants in continuing education seminars, day retreats, and staff development workshops will find this a useful resource. The goal of the text is to start, rather than to conclude, dialogue around the theology of suffering. To that end, each chapter concludes with discussion questions for review and the further exchange of ideas. Finally, each chapter also includes a list of helpful contemporary and classic resources for auxiliary study.

The theological study of suffering and dying is richly rewarding. It invites us to take on directly some of the most frightening and challenging questions and issues all people face. In so doing, we learn about our own levels of comfort and discomfort with mortality (ours and others'); personal spiritual concerns, pains, and questions; and the things that mean most to us in personal and professional life. The study of suffering invites engaged participants into new depths of compassion for ourselves and others. It reminds us of the need for greater humility and tentativeness in theological truth claims. And, it ultimately invites us to live more fully and honestly, as we become more mindful of death asking us always, "How shall you use your time today?"

# 1 Theodicy and the question

## How can God allow pain?

Abba, Father, all things are possible to you. Take this cup away from me, but not what I will but what you will.

Mark 14:36

### Introduction

Jesus' words in the Garden of Gethsemane capture the essence of the dilemma of pain in Christian theology. God is completely powerful; he could spare Jesus the suffering of the Cross. "Take this cup," Jesus pleads. Yet, the Father does not act. Jesus resigns his will to that of the Father, leaving to two millennia of followers the question: does the Father actually *will* this suffering? Was there no other option? The petition of Jesus repeats everywhere there is simultaneously suffering and belief in God. It exists everyday as people pray for this thing that has befallen them to pass. And, everyday, people rationalize their suffering, or the suffering of others, seeking to find meaning yet confounded in resignation that God has somehow willed human pain.

There is a disconnect, even for Jesus,[1] between the reality of suffering and the belief in God. This disconnect comes principally from the notion that God could do something about suffering yet chooses not to act. The divine inaction forces the question of "why?" Is God not powerful enough (and therefore not really God)? Or, is God so powerful that God is beyond good and evil (and therefore not really good)? Or, are human beings so bad that we deserve whatever we get (and therefore God is absolved of all responsibility)?

*Theodicy* is a theological term used to describe the effort to understand God's fundamental nature, complicated by the logical difficulties posed by the reality of evil and suffering. God's nature is understood in the long Christian theological tradition as bearing absolute qualities of power and goodness. Indeed, *Goodness* and *Power* in the absolute sense can be considered synonyms for *God*. The weight of these terms is clarified by thinking about "God" apart from them. Without absolute power, one has to accept a limited conception of God's ability to act. If God cannot intervene, then God must be less powerful than bacteria or a man wielding a club or whatever else it is that ails one. Without absolute goodness, one has to accept a limit to the holiness of God. An all-powerful God that does not care unequivocally about goodness (and does not act in the face of evil) seems more demon than divine.

From a Christian theological perspective, the suggestion of either quality of goodness or lacking omnipotence seems patently erroneous. Yet, if God is all-powerful and all-good as the tradition asserts, why then is there so much suffering? What does suffering say about God's power and goodness? Likewise, what does suffering say about the value of the world when the world is understood as having its genesis in a free act of creation? Could not God have created the world otherwise? Should there not have been some safeguard against suffering or, at the very least, the suffering of innocents?

While such questions can probably never be exhaustively addressed, this chapter intends to introduce some Christian responses to the question of theodicy as I have here described it. The first section offers a brief primer on theological terms used in this text. The next looks at some considerations of personal and corporate suffering. The third section considers the traditional explanation of human sin as the response to the philosophical problem of suffering. The following section considers the theology of the Cross, and the possibility of God's suffering alongside humanity, as a second type of philosophical response to the problem of suffering. Finally, the last section considers some applied aspects of thinking about the meaning of suffering in the face of actual pain. The goal of this chapter is to establish a framework for discussing philosophical interpretations of suffering within a Christian framework and the spiritual issues to which they may give rise. Such a framework is critical in the effort to name and attend to key aspects of intellectual suffering that may lead to faith crisis and in turn compound suffering.

## Brief primer on theological terms

The philosophical considerations of suffering in Christian tradition interweave a number of important theological concepts derived from both the Bible and also the post-biblical tradition of Christian writers. In advancing the discussion, a quick introduction of some basic Christian terms and doctrines will be helpful:

1. *The Bible.* The Christian sacred literature, comprised of the Old Testament and the New Testament.
2. *Christian doctrine of Creation.* This doctrine is important because it anchors the Christian belief that the world comes from God, that life and the world are essentially good, and that all things are in God's providential care.
3. *Christian doctrine of God as Trinity* (or three distinct persons of Father-Son-Holy Spirit in one divine being). This doctrine is important because it can be used to explain how God could experience suffering and death (in the person of the Son) while simultaneously remaining God and extant (in the persons of the Father and Holy Spirit).

4 *Christian doctrine of Jesus' Incarnation, crucifixion and Resurrection.* This doctrine locates the question of human suffering in the life of Jesus of Nazareth (4 BCE–30 CE), believed in the Christian tradition to be both fully human and fully divine. The doctrine of the *Incarnation* purports that God as Son (or second person of the Trinity) became incarnated in humanity, was born of the Virgin Mary, lived a fully human life, and died a real human death in the form of crucifixion. The *Resurrection* is the belief that Jesus was risen to new life (although what manner of new life remains mystery), proving that he was God. This doctrine is important because it underlies the Christian hopes in life beyond death and ultimate justice.
5 *Christian doctrine of human sin, grace, and salvation.* This doctrine explores the human condition as "fallen," while holding at the same time that Jesus' life and death provide correction to that fallenness in the form of grace. This doctrine is important because it suggests that sinful persons, corrected by Jesus' grace, may yet hope for ultimate salvation in the form of one's own resurrection after death.

## Personal and corporate suffering

It is helpful to begin our investigation with the acknowledgment that there are many types of pains in the human life. Some pain is physical (a strained back; an infected tooth; labor in delivery). Physical pain often leads to psychological pain in the form of anxiety and fear (what if the pain in my back is from a malignant tumor? What if I or my child die in childbirth?). The most threatening kind of pain is ultimately the existential, to which all pains invariably give rise (what if I am not strong enough to endure these treatments? Will my children remember me when I am gone? Why was I born in the first place – only to die?).

The potential of existential pain is implicit in the very existence of the human form of life. To the extent that people reflect at all on the human condition, we become aware of the unsettling character of our contingent and limited existences. The experience of ultimate limit contrasts with our individual perceptions of self-definition, personal meaning, and ontological freedom. In the face of the essential limits that death imposes on the human life, we recognize ourselves to be somehow derivative and vulnerable to that from which we are derived. As the great German Jesuit Karl Rahner put it:

> Whenever man in his transcendence experiences himself as questioning, as disquieted by the appearance of being, as open to something ineffable, he cannot understand himself as subject in the sense of an absolute subject, but only in the sense of one who receives being, ultimately only in the sense of grace.[2]

The noble pursuits of truth, beauty, and goodness call us in our finer moments to contemplation of the divine, but it is the limit and vulnerability made obvious by serious illness, or the horror of violence, or the devastation of loss that destabilizes the mundane filter of normalcy and demands attention to both the physical and spiritual natures. Finite, contingent life, in "absolute dependency" in the thought of Friedrich Schleirmacher, leads the human to raise the fundamental theological questions.[3]

Pain that leads to suffering, of course, is not limited to individual experiences. Much, perhaps most, pain in the world is corporate and/or systemic. The past century demonstrates the shocking potential of corporate human suffering in staggering proportions (consider the mass murdering by the Bolsheviks, the incomprehensible scale of the Holocaust, the genocides in Rwanda and Darfur, the tsunamis of the Indian Ocean). Suffering on such a grand scale raises theological questions about the power and goodness of a seemingly reticent and retiring God.

What is more, since the 1960s, a turn to experience as a source and gauge of theological adequacy, characteristic of most liberationist approaches to theology today, adds layers to the concern over corporate suffering viewed through the lens of historical oppression and present struggle. Jon Sobrino, for example, in his article "Theology in a Suffering World," suggests that any theology that is authentically attentive to experience will have to locate itself in the experience of the world's suffering masses.[4] Liberation theologies make explicit the strong connections between the socio-political realities of poverty, slavery, racism, sexism, exploitation, and so on, and the biblical belief that God has some vested interest in the concrete, real-time struggle for human freedom from structures of oppression.

Bringing a theological perspective to socio-political considerations (as well as personal dimensions) of human suffering is risky, and invoking God to explain and justify pain invites potentially devastating spiritual consequences. One thinks here of the biblical prophets, such as Habakkuk. Writing in the sixth century BCE, on the eve of the fall of Jerusalem to the Babylonians, the bewildered prophet complains to God (1:1–4):

> How long, O Lord? I cry for help but you do not listen! I cry out to you, "Violence!" but you do not intervene. Why do you let me see ruin; why must I look at misery? Destruction and violence are before me; there is strife and clamorous discord. This is why the law is benumbed, and judgment is never rendered; because the wicked circumvent the just; this is why judgment comes forth perverted.[5]

In this prophet, God is depicted as sovereign over all people, using the wickedness of one to punish the wickedness of another. Habakkuk represents the human urge: 1) to invoke the name of God to explain and justify one's own suffering as well as the suffering of others; 2) to ask God for deliverance from suffering for self; and 3) to ask God to bring about the (presumably deserved) suffering of one's enemies.[6]

Since the biblical era, and probably long before it, human beings have been tempted to justify actions that bring about the suffering of others in God's name, just as they have confidently attributed to God hurricanes, tsunamis, floods, and all manner of disease.[7] Human beings of all religious persuasions, moreover, postulate of God end-time scenarios, often elaborate, to brace themselves for final suffering and cosmic, apocalyptic warfare.[8] This move consistently leads people to ultimate (and therefore theological) questions of the meaning and reason behind suffering. Indeed, this turn reveals suffering and death as the prime issues that drive the fundamental theological questions about life's meaning.

## The response of sin

Over time, Christians have offered a variety of suggested responses to the questions of suffering and dying. The most frequent classical explanation of suffering is attached to the notion of human sin, derived from the opening chapters of Genesis in the Bible. As depicted in this text, God created a perfect world for human beings, over which they had both power and stewardship:

> God created man in his image; in the divine image he created him; male and female he created them. God blessed them, saying to them: "Be fertile and multiply; fill the earth and subdue it" … "See, I give you every seed-bearing plant all over the earth and every tree that has seed-bearing fruit on it to be your food; and to all the animals of the land, all the birds of the air, and all the living creatures that crawl on the ground, I give all the green plants for food." And so it happened. God looked at everything he had made, and he found it very good.[9]

However, sin, in the form of the human couple's disobedience to God's directives in the Garden of Eden, led to expulsion from paradisiacal living and a series of hard consequences: hard work in tilling land; pain in childbirth; enmity between serpents and people; the first murder. These stories contrast the ideal of blessings and life with the perils of hardship and death, attributing the losses to human responsibility:

> To the woman [God] said: "I will intensify the pangs of your childbearing; in pain you shall bring forth children. Yet your urge shall be for your husband, and he shall be your master." To the man he said: "Cursed be the ground because of you! In toil shall you eat its yield all the days of your life. Thorns and thistles shall it bring forth to you, as you eat the plants of the field. By the sweat of your face shall you get bread to eat. Until you return to the ground from which you were taken; for you are dirt and to dirt you shall return."[10]

For Christians, the perspective that human beings are responsible for their own hardships was succinctly summarized in Paul's Letter to the Romans: "For the wages of sin is death."[11]

In the post-biblical Christian writing, theologians put forth extraordinary efforts at understanding human culpability for sin, the corruption of human free will by sin, and the manner in which pain and suffering serve constructive ends toward redemption from sin. C. S. Lewis' book *The Problem of Pain*[12] represents a twentieth-century appropriation and summarization of this millennia-long theological endeavor.

Lewis responds to the theological problem that pain raises by reconsidering both the notions of God's power and also God's goodness. God's power, Lewis argues, is absolute only in an *originary* sense. This means that God created the universe, complete with natural laws, physical space, and free moral agents (i.e., human beings) to operate within it. God presumably could have created something else or used a different template, but, in fact, God created this world and none other. Within this world, then, once established, God imposed limits (*potentia ordinata*) on God's own limitless power (*potentia absoluta*) in order to allow for genuine freedom for God's creatures. After the original creation, then, God's power is characterized by limits that God self-imposes on Himself.

The effect of this power structure is that it allows for true freedom within creation. If God interfered every time someone wanted to do something wicked, human freedom would quickly disappear. Lewis applies this rationale to the laws of nature as well, providing an explanation (even if an unsatisfying one) for natural disasters and the like. The world of nature has to be fixed and dependable at the physical level if it is to be the arena of free will. A hill cannot flatten just because one person's legs become tired when climbing it; otherwise, no one could ever ski. But, this also means that Jack can fall down and break his crown (or worse, he can be pushed!). In short, the natural world has the potential for suffering insofar as God allows it to be free.

As for God's goodness, Lewis contends that people too easily equate their happiness with goodness. What brings happiness is not always best for people. People are to God as children are to parents (or even pets to owners). Training children (or animals) is not without some discomfort, even pain, to the one being trained. But, a lawless child leads a poor life and is ultimately worse off for having been indulged. Like a parent using discipline, God uses the hardships brought about by natural law and/or human wickedness as didactic tools to refine the spirit. Lewis contends that people turn to God usually when they have nowhere else to turn, and thus Lewis argues that pain serves a complex good in service to spiritual formation.

It is easy for the contemporary person to rebel against this classical solution, largely on the grounds of a gentler model of divine mercy that predominates in the popular theological imagination. But, sin is not a suggestion without some obvious merit. As C. S. Lewis rightly notes, "It is men, not God, who have produced racks, whips, prisons, slavery, guns, bayonets, and bombs; it is by human avarice or human stupidity, not by the churlishness of nature, that we have poverty and overwork."[13] In a related perspective, ecofeminist theologians, such as Catherine Keller and Rosemary Radford Ruether, have variously argued that unchecked human activity is responsible for militarism, war, poverty, overpopulation, and the panoply of environmental hazards associated with pollution, deforestation, land erosion, animal extinction, and related climate and weather pattern changes. In short, they suggest that we may well face an apocalypse, but it is one of human, not divine, doing.[14]

## The response of the Cross

Though intelligible and manifestly, if partially, true, the sin response to the question of pain is inept to answer many human experiences of pain. In the honorable tradition of Job, human beings rightly ask, "What have I done to deserve this?" Or even more, "What have I done for my child to deserve this?" Even though thinkers such as Lewis in the theological tradition might find it plausible to attribute human suffering to some personal error in ourselves or to some original failing in the human species, those who are the bearers of pain often find "sin" an unproductive answer as to why people suffer.

In sympathy with this turn, other Christian writers seek a more satisfying response to pain in the enduring symbol of the Cross. The Cross, like all symbols, reveals its polyvalency in even a terse survey of its meaning over the eras. For some, it is a symbol of conquest over suffering. For others, the Cross is an incentive to endure suffering as means to eventual redemption. For still others, it is a violent symbol of injustice to be resisted and not repeated. Yet for still more, it is a symbol of mediation, hanging as it does between heaven and earth, suggesting new possibilities of forgiveness, friendship, and covenant.

The meaning of the symbol of the Cross is attached to one's basic understanding of God as revealed in the particular history of Jesus of Nazareth. Apart from God, the Cross is merely the wicked end to the life of Jesus, prophet of God, miracle-worker, and holy man of Israel. With God, the Cross is the scandal that raises the question: who is this misunderstood Messiah, the one who must suffer for the redemption of all, the one through whom suffering and dying reveal new possibilities of meaning, purpose, and new life in the face of human meaninglessness, purpose cut short, and mortality?

In the historical effort to understand and even justify the claim that the Messiah of Jewish ancestral hope had to die on the Cross, Christian theologians of the early centuries argued intricately about the relationship of this one, believed now to be risen to glory, and the Father. In their argumentations, they came to articulate an extraordinary claim. In Jesus' human life, God demonstrated God's highest esteem for the human creation by taking into the divine being itself the suffering and dying that is humanity's due course. God, incarnate in the person of Jesus, they held, entered into human life in order to take on and ultimately redeem human pain.[15] In recent writers, such as the German theologian Dorothee Soelle,[16] one finds the argument refined. Although pain persists, humanity is not alone in it. For, God has suffered human pain in the life of Jesus. God is the spirit in the life of the community of salvation, energizing and empowering people to heal and respond to pain in freedom and creativity.

Contemporary author, Douglas John Hall, helps to elucidate the possibilities of reconciling suffering with God. In his work *God and Human Suffering*,[17] Hall explores the logic of suffering by positing two types of suffering in human experience. The first type he names "suffering as becoming." This is the suffering of growth, transformation, yearning, and so on, that is implicit in life lived toward goals, self-betterment, and social progress. This type of suffering is natural to human life and in many ways can be seen as constructive, even good. The irony is that the human motivation "to become" leads to overreaching, pride, greed, and so on, that becomes "suffering as burden," the second type of suffering. The response to the latter type, Hall argues, lies in an internal conversion toward acceptance of the given limits of creaturely existence.

The life (and death) of Jesus models the human call to internal conversion and acceptance of limit. As Hall says of Jesus' Sermon on the Mount, recorded in the Gospel of Matthew 5–7:

> The world that is depicted in it is the world in which we already live and move and have our being. We are not being offered a different world, a supposedly "better" world. We are only being invited to assume a different posture in relation to the world that is already there.[18]

Jesus' humble life meets its end in the agonizing death on the Cross. Yet, maintaining the Christian belief that Jesus is God incarnate, Hall then argues that the Cross becomes the place where God meets human beings in their suffering and even reveals God's own pain. Hall concludes that knowledge of God's participation in human suffering becomes an invitation for people to participate in one another's suffering as a community of redemption. In plainer language, people are called to become the "church" that responds in hope-filled action to the suffering of the world.

Henri-Jérôme Gagey, in his talk "From History to Historicity: The Case of the Resurrection," brings a French, pastoral perspective to this question. Here Gagey argues that Jesus' suffering is the ultimate expression of love that seeks no reward. In love that is ultimately offered even to death, there can be no suspicion of an ulterior motive. Gagey understands that this kind of love is rather senseless and cannot be attached to some more constructive purpose or end. From the critic's perspective, Gagey offers, this is why Christianity is in error – love has no purpose. From the believer's perspective, however, this is the beautiful truth of the faith – love has no purpose. Gagey posits, true love has no ultimate regard for itself, and this is the message of the Cross. What is more, the death of Jesus reveals that love with no self-regard is how God loves humanity. Gagey concludes:

> Here, the cross of the Resurrected one announces that if it is possible to love, this is not to be done as a goal to be attained, nor as a performance waiting for its reward, but, if I may say so, it is done for nothing, not out of duty, not in the hope of becoming righteous or "like a God" (which, one recalls, was Jesus' very own temptation) but solely out of love. This is so because love does not give itself as an objective to be attained but rather as a reality supporting us and making us live.[19]

## Applications

The philosophical problem of suffering and dying is only a problem in light of the belief in God. Without God, it is easy to imagine a violent, natural world in which suffering is given. With God, however, suffering has to be searched and interpreted for the meaning it sheds on both divine and human existence. As considered above, the tradition posits at least two ways of thinking about suffering theologically: 1) human responsibility with suffering as moral corrective; and 2) God enduring suffering alongside humanity. When brought into a dialectic, these responses to the problem of suffering offer rich possibilities for contemplating the human response to pain, personal and corporate, as well as images of the divine that might bolster the human response.

In this fashion, suffering and dying can become focusing tools that orient people to right living and spiritual wholeness. Indeed, the contemplation of death is sometimes called the "*ars moriendi*" (the art of dying). In the *Spiritual Exercises* of Saint Ignatius (1491–1556), the third rule pertaining to the ministry of the distribution of alms captures the essence of this art: "I should picture myself at the hour of my death, and ponder well the way and norm I would then wish to have observed in carrying out the duties of my office."[20]

In other words, one evaluates life and understands the value and correctness of even mundane actions from the point of view of death. To develop this frame of mind is a cultivated art, giving rise to the expression "*ars moriendi, ars vivendi*" (the art of dying is the art of living).

If philosophical contemplation of the problem of suffering invites a more engaged spirituality and conscientious approach to living, what can be said of such contemplation for the person in actual pain, perhaps even facing imminent death? However good they may be, theological answers alone do not sufficiently address pain as it is experienced. Hunger, for example, is most properly met not by explanations of poverty but by food; illness not by tomes but by the loving ministrations of doctors, nurses, and friends. One is reminded here of the contemporary feminist insight that salvation of souls must also involve the *bodies* of the persons being saved.

Such insight invites the searcher to consider the inevitable linkage of spirit and body, a linkage so integral that it is fallacious even to speak as though they were dual aspects of the same reality. That pain is in the end someone's(s') experience, draws us to attend to the particularity of pain. This attending is fruitful. For, just as insight may be gained by looking into the theological tradition for help in understanding pain, so too may looking directly into the experience of pain surface insight to be relayed back to the tradition. The study of pain has edifying implications for the range of systematic theological concerns.

Let me give an example drawn from clinical studies of pain, suffering, palliative care, and end-of-life concerns. A number of key insights quickly emerge from this body of research that may be fruitfully brought to the broader theological dialogue. One very important insight is that physical pain is like a key that naturally unlocks caged spiritual issues. In turn, the spiritual issues take over, redefine, compound, and intensify the person's response to physical pain. Researchers in the area of patient care and pain management find that pain is most effectively managed when a holistic approach to care of persons (as opposed to treatment of patients or, even worse, management of diseases) is modeled.[21]

Patient research also reveals that while people may be committed, ambivalent, or even unconcerned about religion, all people are spiritually engaged. In other words, all people deal with issues of relationship, forgiveness, and meaning. These areas, which require close attention during suffering or at end of life, often overshadow doctrinal approaches to truth. Indeed sometimes doctrinal approaches used to explain suffering or place it within an established worldview are problematic for the person facing end-of-life issues. For example, such issues as estrangement from a church community; difficult history with a minister; lifestyle issues; or even anger at one's Sunday School teacher may lie fallow for years only to provoke crisis in times of illness.

Suffering opens up opportunity and often willingness to repair rifts, restore relationship between the person and God as he or she best conceptualizes the divine, and to forgive. Healing care of a suffering person in this regard is not oriented toward doctrinal teaching or gaining an individual's assent to a set of religious beliefs and such. It is, rather, aimed at eliciting integrative wellness in the suffering person toward the resolution or management of pain in its totality – spiritual, religious, psychological, physical, and so on. In this process, however, religious belief may become deepened, internalized, and more authentically appropriated. Moreover, personal suffering helps to return wisdom and compassion to what may sometimes be merely structural, institutional, and extrinsic religious truth claims. In short, the manner in which we suffer and also care for the suffering of others reveals a great deal about who we are and how adequate our religious belief systems are for support in the journey. Sometimes suffering helps us arrive at better beliefs. Like Jesus in the Gospels, it encourages us to ask, "Who is the Sabbath for?"

## Conclusion

In this chapter we have opened discussion about the meaning of suffering in Christian theology. We have considered in introductory form two models for thinking about God in relationship to the evil of suffering. We have also considered some rudimentary issues related to the application of religious belief to persons in actual pain. Relating the two, if one takes the intimate concerns of the suffering person and returns them to the broader theological questions of theodicy, we discover that an adequate response to thinking about God vis-à-vis the problem of pain will have to include these perennial spiritual issues. A constructive theological investigation driven by caregiving issues related to the theology of suffering is thereby warranted and necessary. It is to deeper consideration of these issues that we now turn.

## Questions for discussion and review

1 How do you define the theological problem of pain?
2 Is it troubling to you to diminish and/or deny the absolute power and/or absolute goodness of God?
3 Enumerate all the ways you can think of in which religion, suffering, and pain intersect.
4 Is "sin" an adequate explanation of human pain and suffering?
5 Can God suffer?

# 2 Suffering in the Bible, Part I

## Old Testament

Lord, my God, I call out by day;
at night I cry aloud in your presence.
Let my prayer come before you;
incline your ear to my cry;
For my soul is filled with troubles;
my life draws near to Sheol.

Psalm 88:1–4

Beloved, do not be surprised that a trial by fire is occurring among you, as if something strange were happening to you. But rejoice to the extent that you share in the sufferings of Christ, so that when his glory is revealed, you may also rejoice exultantly.

1 Peter 4:12–13

## Introduction

The Bible is the most important theological source for Christian faith. Christians of all denominations use the Bible as a foundation for instruction in matters of belief, morality, worship, and spirituality. Christians view the Bible as uniquely able to offer instruction because it is understood to be "sacred" literature. The term "sacred" identifies the Bible as having a special religious quality that makes it essentially different from things that are secular or profane (that is, worldly or common). The special quality is that, according to Christian belief, the Bible comes from God. Many expressions are used to describe how the Bible is thought to come from God. Some include "revelation," "God's word," and "divine inspiration of human authors." Christians of different denominations (such as Orthodox, Catholic, Evangelical, Lutheran, and so on) hold a variety of beliefs about the exact nature of the Bible's sacredness, how it should be read, and how it should be interpreted. Yet, despite differences in how the texts are read and viewed, the Bible is uniformly believed by Christians to be the first and most foundational source of belief and faith.

As the two quotes that open this chapter suggest, Christian faith rooted in the Bible provides a range of resources and perspectives for thinking about the meaning of suffering. The first passage from the Psalms is the opening stanza of a song of lamentation, written from the perspective of a despairing person, reaching out to God for comfort while anticipating the alienation of the grave (Sheol). This passage captures the dialogical, questioning, and sometimes disquieted attitude toward suffering found in the Old Testament. The second passage from the First Letter of Peter represents the attitude toward suffering found in the writings of the New Testament. The Christian community, which was itself struggling in the first century, strove to attach the meaning of the suffering and perils of the human community with the meaning of Jesus' suffering.

The questioning of the Old Testament and the reframed, hopeful attitude in the New Testament are important examples representing the scope of biblical postures toward suffering. To the extent that the Bible is one of the world's oldest and most widely referenced collections of writings for guidance and consolation by suffering persons, it is helpful for caregivers to have some grasp of this biblical material. To that end, this chapter and the next will introduce the reader to suffering and dying in the Old and New Testaments. For each, it will offer a brief primer and historical discussion, followed by a consideration of attitudes toward suffering and dying found in the main subdivisions of the texts.

## Old Testament

The Old Testament (sometimes also called the Hebrew Bible or the First Testament) is a collection of forty-six books (or, thirty-nine, depending on whether one consults a Catholic or Protestant volume), written in Hebrew by the ancient Israelites. If one includes the oral traditions and historical epochs that underlie the present written text, these books span nearly two thousand years of history from 1800 to 100 BCE. The books reflect many changes and developments in Israelite society that occurred over that long expanse of time. It begins with the period of the people as nomadic herders who became enslaved in Egypt (1800–1250 BCE). The historical backdrop carries through the period of the Israelite kingdom (1020–587 BCE), the time of the Babylonian Exile (587–539 BCE), and the restoration of Jerusalem (539–425 BCE). Much of the biblical material was produced during the last five centuries BCE during an extended period of foreign occupation, after the restoration of Jerusalem yet while the Israelites were still under the respective powers of Persia (587–333 BCE), Greece (333–175 BCE), and finally Rome (60 BCE–70 CE). The books of the Old Testament are believed to be sacred by Christians of all church communions as well as by Jews.

As one can imagine, the biblical material produced in such a breadth of time, and under such diverse historical conditions, no doubt by an equally diverse group of authors and editors, represents a comparably broad range of styles, subject matters, and topics. Indeed, one does find many literary genres, points of view, topics, and attitudes. Interestingly, one also finds that attitudes on a single subject often vary from one book to the next, reflecting both differences in the books' authors as well as in the historical contexts and conditions of their particular writing. The major literary genres of the Old Testament include: law; historical books; prophets; and wisdom writings and poetry. Pertinent material in each of these genres contemplates the meaning of suffering and dying. An individual study of each genre will elucidate the span of perspectives the Israelite authors brought to the questions suffering raises.

## Law

There are five books of law in the Old Testament: Genesis, Exodus, Leviticus, Numbers, and Deuteronomy. This collection of books is also referred to by the names *Torah* and *Pentateuch*. Although the books were popularly believed to have been authored singularly by the prophet Moses, scholars in the eighteenth and nineteenth centuries have persuasively argued that the books of the law evidence at least four different authorial voices, ranging from between roughly 1500 and 1000 BCE. These five books tell the tale of Israel's primeval origins and stories of the first matriarchs and patriarchs (Genesis); Israel's period of slavery and exodus from Egypt (Exodus); and Israel's period of wandering in the Sinai desert for a generation while receiving and learning God's covenant law (Exodus, Leviticus, Numbers, and Deuteronomy).

Discussions of suffering and dying in this material are frequent, due in part to the fact that these books interweave life stories with the greater story of God's establishing a covenant with Israel. As such, it is most helpful to identify major themes or arcs in this material, with consideration of some illustrative examples from the text. Although one could identify others, themes I would like to focus on here include: 1) natural, human life; 2) mortality wrought by sin and disobedience; 3) covenant; and 4) communal responsibility – punishment and reward:

1 *Natural, human life*. In the books of the law, readers find interesting stories of Israel's founding figures, such as: Adam and Eve; Noah and his family; Abraham and Sarah; Isaac and Rebekah; and Jacob along with his two wives and two concubines; Moses; Joshua; and others. The number of years of life given to these figures is frequently exaggerated as a storytelling device to emphasize their importance and blessedness by God. An average lifespan was forty years, yet, for example, Noah is said to have lived 950 years (Gen. 9:29). Despite the great ages, one of the first remarkable things about these figures is that they are not actually that unique or remarkable. They are depicted as people with regular hopes, dreams, fears, and disappointments. They desire children and celebrate healthy births. They sometimes use poor judgment, make mistakes, and mistreat one another. They bury their loved ones and grieve death. They are not the demigods of the Greek myths, like Hercules and Achilles. They do not rise from the grave when they pass away nor hope for life after death. Their hopes are centered on marriage, offspring, good pasturing for their flocks, and finding food and water. Sometimes they demonstrate a new level of trust or a novel response

to God's summons, as in the case with Abraham, Isaac, and Jacob. In this sense, they cooperate with God in unexpected ways that advance the story. In most respects, however, their lives are fairly typical of their era and location, set against a semi-nomadic, trader-caravan milieu. This depiction of human life is very naturalistic, with the focus being on life lived as abundantly as possible. Death is regarded as an end of life and an end to the personal trajectories of individual existence; God's blessing is seen in the survival of the community and in fecundity lived out from one generation to the next.

2 *Mortality wrought by sin and disobedience*. Where one finds a focus on suffering and death in the law, it will typically surround human agents acting sinfully and disobediently toward God. The introduction of death in the Old Testament comes early, in the third chapter of Genesis. This chapter tells the tale of the fall of the human couple and their expulsion from paradise. When Adam and Eve disobey God by eating the forbidden fruit, their punishments include hard work toiling the land, pain in childbirth, and mortality. The story is best understood as a tale the Israelites told to explain why work is hard and life is brief. It is interesting to note, however, that despite the failing of the couple, God is depicted as nevertheless providential and concerned about human welfare. For example, when Adam and Eve feel shame at their nakedness, God weaves them little garments of leaves to cover themselves. The motif of God at once allowing penalty for human sin while simultaneously meeting human need and loss with compassion repeats throughout the books of the law.

3 *Covenant*. Perhaps the best example of God's compassionate response to human sin in these books is the establishment of the covenant with the people of Israel. The first mention of covenant in the Bible comes in Genesis 9, which recounts the story of God's pact with Noah (sealed by the sign of the rainbow in the sky) that God will never again destroy the earth with a flood. Of course, earlier in the story, God brings about a near apocalyptic flood in response to human wickedness. But here, at the resolution of the story, God is depicted as merciful and beneficent. No matter what people will do, God will never again destroy them. This covenant, established first with Noah, provides in the Pentateuch the basis for the ongoing relationship between God and the people, enacted under the leadership of Israel's great matriarchs and patriarchs (Abraham and Sarah; Isaac and Rebekah; Jacob and his family; and Moses).

Beginning with Abraham, the biblical language suggests that God "remembers" the covenant he established with people. Especially when they get into trouble, God remembers his relationship and emerges to mitigate and correct their suffering. The most prominent example of this is the story of deliverance of the Israelite people from enslavement in Egypt (an event known as the *exodus* and relayed in the book of Exodus). Here God uses the full power of nature in order to sway the king of Egypt to release the people from captivity. Upon their release, Moses leads the Israelites into the desert where God miraculously provides food and water for them. In the greatest event in the Book of Exodus, God meets Moses face-to-face and gives him the covenant law. The law has many different types of duties and obligations attached to it, aimed at establishing just relationships among people and right relationship between the people and God. All human blessing and suffering, then, comes to be seen as what it is in light of the law. Blessing, life, fertility, and so on, are the outcome of right relationship with God; conversely, suffering, death, defeat, and so on, are the outcome of violating the relationship with God. The covenant is not optional, as though the people could find alternative forums for living out their existence. Rather, the covenant relationship between people and God becomes the interpretive framework for making sense of life's ups and downs.

4 *Communal responsibility*. Contrasting with more individualistic models characteristic of today's affluent societies, the Israelites were semi-nomadic herders who lived communally in large kin-groups and clan networks. They experienced en masse the actions and repercussions of individuals. As such, the covenant in the Pentateuch is depicted as something that is lived out communally. Blessings are enjoyed by the whole; suffering (even if it is earned by a single individual's sinfulness) ripples throughout family, clan, and tribe. Moreover, the blessing and suffering experienced by the community is depicted as bestowed by God in recognition respectively of righteousness and fidelity *or* injustice and sacrilege.

## Historical books

The historical books of the Old Testament are: Joshua, Judges, 1 and 2 Samuel, 1 and 2 Kings, 1 and 2 Chronicles, Ezra, Nehemiah, Tobit, Judith, Esther, and 1 and 2 Maccabees. This collection of books, composed over several hundred years, tells the story (spanning roughly 1000–100 BCE) of the Israelite settlement of the land of Canaan, the kingdoms of Israel and Judah, the Babylonian Exile, the Restoration of Judah, and occupation under Assyria, Babylon, Persia, and Greece. A discussion of suffering in these books must by necessity take into consideration the vantage point of the historical oppressions associated with foreign occupation. When the history of conquest, exile, and occupation in the historical books is juxtaposed with the stories of covenant and law in the Pentateuch, an interesting perspective on suffering emerges. The Israelites were forced to ask the question: why? Why should a people of the covenant – specially chosen by God for deliverance from slavery in Egypt and deeded by God the land of Canaan – why should these people suffer the burdens of enemies at their borders, defeat in battle, exile into foreign lands, and centuries of occupation? The belief in having been selected by God and the reality of historical violence produced the phenomenon of profound, corporate self-critique. This self-critique is especially pronounced due to the feature that the historical books were edited (or redacted) not at the beginning of Israel's kingdom but at its end (like a person composing a life-review from a hospice bed).

Adding to this perspective is the backdrop of Canaanite and Israelite religion, in which animal (and sometimes human) sacrifice played a key role. The covenant law of the Israelites describes in great detail types of sacrifices required for various intents and purposes: thanksgiving; sin; atonement. Sacrifice served as the mechanism by which people: 1) praised God by returning the gift of life back to its source; and 2) restored or repaired breaches with God caused by error and wickedness. Furthermore, sacrifice was done at the level of both individual and society, reflecting again the emphasis on communal, religious life.

In light of the combined features of a sacrificial cultural mindset and corporate, self-critique, the distinctive picture of Israel's sense of suffering in history comes into view. When one reads the historical books, one sees the qualities of nostalgia, loss, and self-reproach alongside aspirations for greatness, an enduring sense of promise, and the hope of future restoration. The former qualities constitute the community's self-evaluation of how and why God would allow them to suffer defeat and loss so brutally. The historical writers reasoned God was punishing Israel for breaking the covenant law by practicing religious infidelity (worshiping gods other than Yahweh) and by failure to act socially in just and moral ways. The latter qualities constitute the community's belief that God is ultimately good, just, and in control over the whole natural order. Although God may allow for punishment, sometimes on a devastating scale, they advanced the argument that God in turn would punish those who hurt Israel. They developed hope in a final restoration for those who were repentant and faithful to God.

Both of these sets of qualities are evidenced in the late historical tale of the martyrdom of an Israelite mother and her seven sons under the cruel treatment of the Seleucid overlord Antiochus IV Epiphanes in the second century BCE, recounted in 2 Maccabees 7. In this exemplary passage, one reads of the systematic torture and murder of seven children before the eyes of their mother. The mother watches six of her sons be maimed, scalped, and burned alive. As her seventh child is called forth, Antiochus devises yet a worse fate for him, namely, that he should abandon his beliefs and enter into prestigious service in the tyrant's court. The courageous mother, believing firmly that this present suffering is fleeting, encourages him in his native Hebrew tongue to hold firm. She exhorts (2 Maccabees 7:20–23 and 27–29):

> I do not know how you came into existence in my womb; it was not I who gave you the breath of life, nor was it I who set in order the elements of which each of you is composed. Therefore, since it is the Creator of the universe who shapes each man's beginning, as he brings about the origin of everything, he, in his mercy, will give you back both breath and life, because you now disregard yourselves for the sake of his laws ... Son, have pity on me, who carried you in my womb for nine months, nursed you for three years, brought you up, educated and supported you to your present age. I beg you child to look to the heavens and the earth and see all that is

> in them; then you will know that God did not make them out of existing things, and in the same way the human race came into existence. Do not be afraid of this executioner, but be worthy of your brothers and accept death, so that in the time of mercy I may receive you again with them.

The son, inspired by his mother's word, turns to his tormenter and says (2 Maccabees 7:30–38):

> What are you waiting for? I will not obey the king's command. I obey the command of the law given to our forefathers through Moses. But you, who have contrived every kind of affliction for the Hebrews, will not escape the hands of God. We, indeed, are suffering because of our sins. Though our living lord treats us harshly for a little while to correct us with chastisements, he will again be reconciled with his servants. But you, wretch, vilest of all men! do not, in your insolence, concern yourself with unfounded hopes, as you raise your hand against the children of Heaven. You have not escaped the judgment of the almighty and all-seeing God. My brothers, after enduring brief pain, have drunk of never-failing life, under God's covenant, but you, by the judgment of God, shall receive just punishment for your arrogance. Like my brothers, I offer up my body and my life for our ancestral laws, imploring God to show mercy soon to our nation, and by afflictions and blows to make you confess that he alone is God. Through me and my brothers, may there be an end to the wrath of the Almighty that has justly fallen on our whole nation.

In this equally exemplary passage, one finds summarized the attitude toward suffering in the historical books characterized by the themes of:

- the covenant that binds the people to God
- punishment for disobeying God's law
- reward for obeying God's law
- God's justice in using human agents to do God's corrective will
- hope for reconciliation with God after punishment that is duly given
- hope for a final restoration, characterized here as unfailing life after death
- sacrifice, depicted here as the death of the brothers to earn God's mercy for the nation
- and finally, a general emphasis on national, rather than personal, interests.

## Prophets

The books of the prophets include Isaiah, Jeremiah, Lamentations, Baruch, Ezekiel, Daniel, Hosea, Joel, Amos, Obadiah, Jonah, Micah, Nahum, Habakkuk, Zephaniah, Haggai, Zechariah, and Malachi. These books span the eighth through the fifth centuries BCE, paralleling the stories of Israel's kingdoms found in the historical books mentioned above. Far from being fortune-tellers, Israel's prophets functioned rather as spokespersons who conveyed important theological messages to the people and the leaders of Israel and Judah. These messages came as visions, as oracles of woe, as images of hope, even as symbolic gestures meant to rally attentive listeners to God's exhortations. As with before, most of the prophetic messages have to do with communal life and the welfare of the nation. In other words, messages are not directed at individuals for private purposes. Having said that, it is the conduct of individuals, from the level of the highest king to that of the merchant in the market place, toward which the prophets bring their scrutinizing speech.

What were the important theological messages that the prophets proclaimed? They assessed whether and how well the community, and especially the leaders of the community, kept the laws of the covenant established for Israel at the time of Exodus. For, it was on the basis of the covenant law that Israel existed at all. As such, if and when Israel broke its covenant obligations, the people were subject to punishment and correction. The prophets served to warn the people against defiling the covenant, to chastise them in the face of wrongdoing, to proclaim forthcoming disaster in the wake of evil, and finally to give hope for restoration after the fact. Sometimes the prophets spoke directly to the kings of Israel and Judah; other times the prophets directed their messages more generally to the people as a whole. Their prophecies detail the context and the outcomes of the numerous tragic episodes in the kingdoms' history, including prominently: the Assyrian conquest of Israel in 722 BCE; the Babylonian conquest and exile of Judah in 586 BCE; and the restoration of Judah as a vassal of Persia in 539 BCE.

The works of the prophets are especially helpful in illustrating the Old Testament attitudes toward suffering and death insofar as they expertly articulate the model of sin, punishment, sacrifice, forgiveness, and restoration to holiness already mentioned. More importantly, however, a comparison of the prophetic voices demonstrates that Israel's interpretation of suffering was flexible and developmental in response to differing historical contexts. A few examples will be helpful here: Amos, Jeremiah, and Ezekiel.

Amos was a prophet who spoke in the northern kingdom of Israel during the reign of King Jeroboam II in 786–746 BCE. During this time, Israel was prospering yet blind to the growing threat of the Assyrian armies to the east. In vanity, Israel succumbed to the indulgences of prosperity. In the words of Amos, the rich are "storing up in their castles on the mountainsides the wealth they extorted and robbed" (3:10). The high-class women lounge about on couches, demanding from their lords to be served drinks. They are accused of "oppressing the weak" and "abusing the needy" (4:1). These same people come to the public shrines and make a grand show of their sacrifices and offerings while accepting bribes, behaving unjustly, and repelling the needy at their gates (5:12). Moreover, they have ignored the signs God has placed before them as warnings about their ways – drought, searing winds, animal pestilence (4:7–10). This rampant social injustice represents for Amos the principal sacrilege and abuse of the covenant, evidenced most in the superficiality of their religious observances. Proclaiming on God's behalf, Amos cries (5:21–24):

> I hate, I spurn your feasts, I take no pleasure in your solemnities; your cereal offerings I will not accept, nor consider your stall-fed peace offerings. Away with your noisy songs! I will not listen to the melodies of your harps. But if you would offer me holocausts [i.e., burnt offerings], then let justice surge like water, and goodness like an unfailing stream.

Amos goes on to proclaim the forthcoming demise of Israel. Much as he anticipated, Israel was indeed destroyed by Assyria only two decades after Amos prophesied. What one observes in this prophet is an extreme anger directed against social injustices and vain displays of religion. As these are direct violations of the covenant, Amos foresees that the kingdom will lose God's blessing, incur God's wrath, and not long endure. In such a context, the suffering of the well-to-do is depicted as earned punishment for the suffering in others that they themselves have caused.

Jeremiah, a later prophet, presents a gentler side of suffering in the face of God's justice. Jeremiah lived and worked in the southern kingdom of Judah in the late seventh and early sixth centuries BCE. His career spanned the important reign of King Josiah, who launched a thoroughgoing religious reform in Judah in 628 BCE. Jeremiah endorsed the reform efforts, but saw them die unfinished along with Josiah himself from a battle wound in 609 BCE. In the three decades that followed Josiah's death, Jeremiah saw Judah return to idolatrous ways. He subsequently witnessed the rise of Babylon, the sack of Jerusalem under the Babylonian king Nebuchadnezzar, the destruction of the temple in Jerusalem, and the exile of the citizens of Judah. Jeremiah's book is the testimony of a man who proclaims God's word in these circumstances as well as the record of the personal struggles that befall one called to prophesy under such tumult.

Believing that the people deserve punishment, Jeremiah nevertheless pleads with God for mercy on account of mankind's basic frailty (Jeremiah 10:23–25):

> You know, O Lord, that man is not master of his way; man's course is not within his choice, nor is it for him to direct his step. Punish us, O Lord, but with equity, not in anger, lest you have us dwindle away. Pour out your wrath on the nations that know you not, on the tribes that call upon your name; for they have devoured Jacob [i.e., Israel] utterly and laid waste his dwelling.

Jeremiah, further, expresses frustration at his own frailty and limitation. He feels an ineluctable call to prophesy God's messages, and he responds to that call with intensity and commitment. Yet, he is not rewarded for his work. The people of Judah do not want to hear his messages of doom, and God seemingly does nothing to ease his burden. Unabashedly, Jeremiah complains to God about the hardships of persecution and thankless work:

> Woe to me, mother, that you gave me birth! A man of strife and contention to all the land! I neither borrow nor lend, yet all curse me. Tell me, Lord, have I not served you for their good? Have I not interceded with you in the time of misfortune and anguish? You know I have. Remember me, Lord, visit me, and avenge me on my persecutors … why is my pain continuous, my wound incurable, refusing to be healed? You have indeed become for me a treacherous brook whose waters do not abide!

Having watched the people of Jerusalem slain or bound and driven away in chains, Jeremiah continues to prophesy by reaching out to the exiles in letters. He attempts to encourage them now, no longer prophesying their downfall but rather prophesying their restoration. He heartens them to be industrious, to marry and reproduce, and to pray for the good of their new city of residence (Jeremiah 29). Though decades will pass, Jeremiah instills in them hope in the face of their suffering as he conveys God's promise of renewal (Jeremiah 33:3–9):

> "Call to me, and I will answer you; I will tell you things great beyond reach of knowledge." Thus says the Lord, the God of Israel, concerning the houses of this city and the palaces of Judah's kings, which are being destroyed in the face of siegeworks and the sword … "Behold, I will treat and assuage the city's wounds; I will heal them, and reveal to them an abundance of lasting peace. I will change the lot of Judah and the lot of Israel and rebuild them as of old. I will cleanse them of all the guilt they incurred by sinning against me; all their offences by which they sinned and rebelled against me, I will forgive. Then Jerusalem shall be my joy, my praise, my glory, before all the nations of the earth, as they hear of all the good I will do among them. They shall be in fear and trembling over all the peaceful benefits I will give her."

In the passages considered here, one sees in Jeremiah a tender vision of hope and also frustration over the lot of humanity. The people are vulnerable to their own shortcomings, punishments, and even to the love of God. Jeremiah captures the element of *dialogue* between the people and God on the question of suffering, which one finds repeated in other prophetic works (for example, Habakkuk and Micah). In other passages in Jeremiah, one finds a shifting perspective on the meaning of covenant and responsibility. Jeremiah prophesies "a new covenant," one which will now be "within them" and "written upon their hearts." For, he prophesies, "I will be their God, and they shall be my people" (31:33). He further suggests that the exiles will no longer bear the responsibility of their forefathers' sins. In exile, separated from the land, the kingdom, and the temple, the covenant can no longer be viewed as a matter of laws binding the state, the priests and kings. The teaching now becomes an internalized relationship between the people and God, which can be lived or experienced even in bondage.

The last prophet to be considered here is Ezekiel, who strongly echoes Jeremiah's sentiments. Ezekiel is unique among prophets because he lived and worked outside of Jerusalem among the exiles in Babylon from 593 to 571 BCE. His purpose is to prophesy a combined message of repentance and forgiveness to the people cast away from their homes. Ezekiel delivers a number of prophecies against the foreign nations who have harmed Israel, and he follows these prophecies with powerful visions about a revised moral code and the hope for a restored Jerusalem. The prophecies against foreign nations help to explain to the exiles why they suffer so. God used Israel's enemies to convey a strong message to wayward Israel; but, this does not mean that the enemies will not in turn pay for their own crimes. Suffering is here understood as earned but restricted by God's overarching sense of balance and justice.

The belief that suffering is earned, however, must here also be reconsidered in light of the scope and nature of the people's loss. Many of the exiles would have been mere children at the time of the Babylonian conquest. Many Israelites were born in exile, while many others died there. Many of Ezekiel's audience, no doubt, would have had a difficult time owning the burden of crimes committed by long-deceased forefathers from a far-away homeland they had never seen. Ezekiel therefore prophesies that the old moral code of communal responsibility was now to be replaced with a new teaching. For the exiles, he says, "the son shall not be charged with the guilt of his father, nor shall the father be charged with the guilt of his son. The virtuous man's virtue shall be his own, as the wicked man's wickedness shall be his" (Ezekiel 18:20). In a similar vein, he concludes, "Cast away from you all the crimes you have committed, and make yourselves a new heart and a new spirit" (Ezekiel 18:31).

Imbued with a new spirit, the exiles were free to live with a clean slate and a new sense of covenant. In chapter 37, Ezekiel envisions this new covenant in dramatic terms. In one memorable vision, Ezekiel is swept away to the middle of a plain filled with skeletal remains. The bones represent the lost nations of Israel and Judah. At God's behest, Ezekiel speaks to the bones, telling them to come to life. As he does so, the bones begin to rattle, join together, form connective tissue, and grow flesh. Then, Ezekiel is commanded to prophesy to them that spirit shall fill them and bring them to life. At his words, the bones become a vast army of resurrected Israelites. While Ezekiel's prophecy principally predicts the restoration of the nation, its powerful image of resurrected bodies becomes fodder for a new kind of hope. Not only may the suffering exiles hope for a restored kingdom; they may also now hope for resurrected life after their own personal deaths. This image is immediately followed by Ezekiel's promise of an everlasting covenant of peace (37:26). Herein, one finds the first intermingling in the Old Testament of this worldly hope for a new kingdom with other worldly hope for eternal life.

As a whole, the prophets achieve a skillful explanation of suffering. It is earned by human sin but circumscribed by God's mercy. It is an occasion for moral correction and renewal. And, renewal will be better than the original condition that led to the suffering.

## Wisdom writings and poetry

The wisdom writings and poetry books include: Job, Psalms, Proverbs, Ecclesiastes, Song of Songs, Wisdom, and Sirach. Unlike the books of law, history, and prophecy, the wisdom books do not deal explicitly with Israel's history or its woes as a nation. These books, rather, take up directly what the others do indirectly. Namely, they openly explore the meaning of life. They consider love and loss; work and play; happiness and sorrow; life and death. There is a refreshing, skeptical quality to many of these writings insofar as they are not obviously pious. On matters of suffering, they do not offer easy answers, or even answers at all. Rather, these ancient texts (composed throughout Israel's long history) ask alongside readers of every era perennial questions about the purpose of life in the face of death. Key among the wisdom writings that directly consider suffering are the Psalms, Ecclesiastes, and the Book of Job.

The Psalms is a book of 150 poems. The poems were likely used as sung elements of the liturgy during religious gatherings. They span hundreds of years in composition and cover a range of topics, including praise of Yahweh, praise of the king, and lamentations. The consideration of suffering in the Psalms represents an integration of the major themes on suffering found in the law, the history, and the prophets. For example, Psalm 137, written by the exiles in Babylon, expresses the depth of loss the authors have experienced as well as hope for retribution against Israel's enemies. The national loss of the exiles is achingly captured in tones that shift from nostalgic, to self-recriminating, to vengeful, all of which are brought to God in prayer:

> By the rivers of Babylon
> we sat mourning and weeping
> when we remembered Zion.
> On the poplars of that land
> we hung our harps.
> There our captors asked us
> for the words of a song;
> our tormentors, for a joyful song;
> "Sing for us a song of Zion!"
> But how could we sing a song of the Lord
> in a foreign land?
>
> If I forget you, Jerusalem,
> may my right hand wither.

May my tongue stick to my palate
if I do not remember you.
If I do not exalt Jerusalem
beyond all my delights.

Remember, Lord, against Edom
that day at Jerusalem.
They said: "Level it, level it
down to its foundations!"
Fair Babylon, you destroyer,
happy those who pay you back
the evil you have done us!
Happy those who seize your children
and smash them against a rock.

Similar themes are found in the intimate tones of personal distress found in Psalm 143:

Lord, hear my prayer;
in your faithfulness listen to my pleading.
Answer me in your justice.
Do not enter into judgment with your servant
before you no living being can be just.
The enemy has pursued me;
they have crushed my life to the ground.
They have left me in darkness like those long dead.
My spirit is faint within me;
my heart is dismayed.
I remember the old days;
I ponder all your deeds;
the works of your hands I recall.
I stretch out my hands to you;
I thirst for you like a parched land.
Hasten to answer me, Lord,
for my spirit fails me.
Do not hide your face from me,
lest I become like those descending to the pit.
At dawn let me hear your kindness,
for in you I trust.
Show me the path I should walk,
for to you I entrust my life.
Rescue me, Lord, from my foes,
for in you I hope.
Teach me to do your will,
for you are my God.

May your kind spirit guide me
on the ground that is level.
For your name's sake, Lord, give me life;
in your justice lead me out of distress.
In your kindness put an end to my foes;
destroy all who attack me,
For I am your servant.

If the Psalms are rife with prayer for solace and meaning in the face of suffering, the Book of Ecclesiastes presents a skeptical perspective on the question of life's meaning. Written sometime in the fourth century BCE, the book openly questions the value of human life. Although the author expresses trust in a divine plan, human beings cannot know it and therefore are saddled with uncertainty and vain struggle. The joy in anything and everything is tainted by awareness of its fleetingness and questionable value. Ecclesiastes brings under the searchlight of his critique a discussion of the vanity of all things: the acquisition of wealth; the pursuit of wisdom; the value of companions and successors; the quest for justice; the desire for pleasure and enjoyment; the benefit of gain; and even the sensibility of sorrow over loss. Everything under the sun, the author concludes, is vain chasing after wind. We do not know what evil lurks around the corner, he notes, and a well-lived life comes to the same end as a poorly lived one. There are certain advantages, the author consents, to the value of hard work, and wisdom has the advantage over folly as light has over darkness. But, the best a person can do is to try to enjoy a just day's wage, a decent meal, and a good night's sleep because "the days of darkness will be many. All that is to come is vanity" (Ecclesiastes 11:7).

The dissatisfied conclusions of Ecclesiastes represent a key element of the wisdom writings on the question of suffering. The Old Testament authors do not gloss over the frustration and anger to which loss and limit give rise. A sense of confusion and ambiguity about life's meaning are held side-by-side with a trust (or at least the desire to trust) that God is actually in charge, that the universe does make sense, and that justice will prevail. The Book of Job brings to full measure these questions, thus earning its place as one of the world's greatest literary treatments of the meaning of suffering. Likely written sometime between the seventh and fifth centuries BCE, this book is a didactic dialogue questioning such themes as suffering, innocence, righteousness, punishment, divine goodness, and divine power.

In the dialogue, Job is presented as a righteous man, whose goodness is proven in the abundant blessings of prosperity and wealth that Job enjoys. In the prologue to the story, Satan (the courtroom adversary) approaches God on the question of whether Job would be so faithful a man if he were stripped of his blessings. God permits Satan to wreck Job's fortune, bringing death to his children and destruction to his wealth, property, and livestock. Yet unharmed physically, Job continues to bless God, for he believes "the Lord gave and the Lord has taken away" (Job 1:21). Satan then presses the issue. What happens when Job's own health is ruined? Will he still continue to bless God? Now Job becomes smitten with boils and sickness. He is reduced to a shadow of a man, bereft of everything, scraping his sores among the ashes.

The dialogue ensues between Job and his three interlocutors (Eliphaz, Bildad, and Zophar). When his friends approach Job, one would expect them to offer words of condolence but instead they bring reproach, representing the wisdom of the day. "Job," they query in essence, "what have you done to make God so angry with you?" When Job replies that he is innocent, they charge further that Job is not only sinful but also arrogant and blasphemous. For, of course, they suggest, God does nothing undeserved. If people suffer, it is because they have earned it and ought to repent. Job, however, protests his innocence. As with most people when tragedy strikes on such an order of magnitude, Job cannot conceive of any sin in himself so great as to merit this boundless suffering. Thus, even while Job challenges God to answer why he must suffer so, Job maintains before his friends the dual conviction that God is just and that he himself is actually an innocent man. "Let God weigh me in the scales of justice; thus he will know my innocence!" (Job 31:6).

The power of the dialogue lies in part in the unabashed manner in which Job protests his situation. He becomes a voice for everyone who suffers in his certainty that he cannot possibly have merited the deaths of his children, the ruination of his own body, and the loss of his wealth and good name. But, the three interlocutors have raised an important point: can anyone claim to be truly righteous? Late in the dialogue Elihu, a fourth interlocutor, joins the conversation. He raises the point that Job's suffering is corrective, serving to draw Job nearer to God. "[M]an is chastened on his bed by pain and unceasing suffering within his frame" (Job 33:19), so that when he is weakened as a child (Job 33:26–28):

> He shall pray and God will favor him; he shall see God's face with rejoicing. He shall sing before men and say, "I sinned and did wrong, yet he has not punished me accordingly. He delivered my soul from passing to the pit, and I behold the light of life."

Until chapter 38, the book offers varied points of view, presented as a human investigation into the experience of suffering and God's (in)justice. The dramatic turn then occurs when God himself joins the dialogue. Having been challenged directly by Job to explain suffering, God now turns the question back to Job, "Who is this that obscures divine plans with words of ignorance? Gird up your loins now, like a man; I will question you, and you will tell me the answers" (Job 38:2). The Lord proceeds to ask Job such questions as whether Job controls the snow and hail for days of battle; where Job was when the foundation of the world was laid; how Job assists the mountain goats when they give birth; if it was Job who set the constellations in the sky; and whether it is by Job's power that the hawk soars in the sky. By lambasting Job with rhetorical questions that he can in no way answer, God demonstrates a power over the cosmos that evades human understanding. Of course, God does not answer Job's question about suffering, but rather God's queries reframe the whole dialogue. Human suffering occurs within a world and a cosmos. It is a part of a greater whole that is incomprehensible at the creaturely level. The encounter with God relativizes Job's point of view, leading him to repent from his anger and puzzlement over his suffering: "I had heard of you by word of mouth, but now my eye has seen you. Therefore I disown what I have said, and repent in dust and ashes" (Job 42:5–6). The dialogue concludes with God restoring to Job his health, his wealth, and children, double what he had before. It leaves, however, the reader searching: do new children replace the ones who were killed? Is God good, or just Almighty? Must people meet God in their suffering and in their innocence in order to know God personally? Job provides no easy answers.

## Conclusion

The Old Testament authors provide a rich and varied dialogue on the question of human suffering. The backdrop of the biblical discussion is largely national and political. As a result, the consideration of suffering is frequently undertaken in light of national and political interests: why does the nation suffer defeat? Why does the king permit injustice? Why have the people been exiled? And so on. The questions are raised further against the belief that God chose the Israelites to be a special people uniquely bound to God by their covenant. The experience of national suffering combined with belief in the covenant became for the Israelites the framework for their interpretation of suffering as either brought about or permitted by God as a response and corrective to human sin. This model of sin/punishment and faithfulness/reward offered a viable explanation for experience at the levels of personal and national interests. Yet, while the explanation was persuasive and certainly holds sway in the historical, legal, and prophetic writings, the wisdom writings bring a more nuanced perspective to the question of human suffering. In the wisdom materials, one finds the authors searching (sometimes even impatiently) for answers. As prayer, these writings convey a tenor of hope and trust even while they admit feelings of frustration, fear, and skepticism.

For individuals who believe that the writings of the Old Testament are sacred, these combined resources provide useful material to reflect on suffering in the present day. The trust in God's providence and justice is blended with a realistic attitude of uncertainty that often crops up in the experience of suffering. The national as well as personal tones are helpful resources for people contemplating not only the intimate experience of suffering but also the grand scale of suffering experienced in war, political oppression, and natural disaster. One finds the biblical authors bringing the whole range of their experience to God in prayer, and their quest for understanding meets empathetic readers across time and culture. Particularly poignant is the quest itself. The power of this material to ameliorate suffering lies in the ability of these ancient voices to articulate the questions as if people today were speaking them. In this way, they remind readers of all times and cultures that they are not alone in their journeys.

## Questions for review and discussion

1 What are the four main divisions in the Old Testament literature? How does each characterize the reality of suffering?
2 How does this literature communicate suffering at both the corporate and personal levels? Do you think it helps lessen the suffering of individuals to consider the suffering of others?
3 How might the skepticism of these texts be a benefit or hindrance to individuals who are suffering?
4 What, if any, experiences have you had with this literature that shape how you read and understand it?

## Resources

*Jewish Study Bible*. Oxford: Oxford University Press, 2004.
*Saint Mary's Press College Study Bible*. Winona, Minnesota: Saint Mary's Press, 2007.
Blenkinsopp, Joseph. *Wisdom and Law in the Old Testament: Ordering of Life in Israel and Early Judaism*. New York: Oxford University Press, 1995.
Boadt, Lawrence. *Introduction to Wisdom Literature*. Collegeville, Minnesota: The Liturgical Press, 1986.
Carvalho, Corrine. *Encountering Ancient Voices: A Guide to Reading the Old Testament*. Winona, Minnesota: Saint Mary's Press, 2006.
Ceresko, Anthony R. *Introduction to Old Testament Wisdom: A Spirituality for Liberation*. Maryknoll, New York: Orbis Books, 1999.
Coggins, R. J. *Introducing the Old Testament*. New York: Oxford University Press, 1990.
Wensing, Michael G. *Death and Destiny in the Bible*. Collegeville, Minnesota: The Liturgical Press, 1993.

# 3 Suffering in the Bible, Part II

## New Testament

> Two blind men were sitting by the roadside, and when they heard that Jesus was passing by, they cried out, "Lord, Son of David, have pity on us!" The crowd warned them to be silent, but they called out all the more, "Lord, Son of David, have pity on us!" Jesus stopped and called them and said, "What do you want me to do for you?" They answered him, "Lord, let our eyes be opened." Moved with pity, Jesus touched their eyes. Immediately they received their sight, and followed him.
>
> Matthew 20:30–34

> Behold, we are going up to Jerusalem, and the Son of Man will be handed over to the chief priests and scribes. And they will condemn him to death and hand him over to the Gentiles who will mock him, spit upon him, scourge him, and put him to death, but after three days he will rise.
>
> Mark 10:33–34

### Introduction

The New Testament is a collection of twenty-seven books produced in the ancient Greek language by early Christian writers roughly between the years 50 and 110 CE. The books of the New Testament are the principal sources Christians have for learning about the life of Jesus and his earliest followers. Like the books of the Old Testament, the New Testament books represent different literary genres, authors, background contexts, and dates of composition. The books present different emphases and points of view on the life of Jesus, and they together provide a dynamic picture of the developing first-century community that gave birth to the Christian religion.

At its inception, this community was an offshoot sect of Judaism. Jesus himself was a Jewish man, steeped in the Jewish culture, law, and literary heritage. From the Hebraic perspective, the life and death of Jesus were read through the interpretive framework of past Jewish history and writings (considered in Chapter Two). Within a matter of decades, however, Gentile (or non-Jewish) converts predominantly populated the Christian movement. These Gentiles brought a Greco-Roman cultural and philosophical framework to the interpretation of Jesus' life and death. The New Testament writings, therefore, are best understood in light of the blending and sometimes competing trajectories of Jewish and Gentile contexts, histories, and philosophical predispositions.

In both the Jewish and Gentile contexts, the question of suffering loomed large. The Roman Empire was vast in its expanse and power, but life was hard and often brief under imperial rule. In the particular context of occupied Judaea (modern-day Israel), in which the events of Jesus' life took place, common people were subject to high taxation, servitude, and brutal demonstrations of the power of the state and Roman military. Moreover, for the masses living conditions were poor: cramped dwellings; lack of sanitation and waste disposal; frequent fires and building collapses; and risk of criminal violence. For the emergent Christian population, the risks of everyday life were compounded by government suspicion and regular outbreaks of persecution against the new religious movement.[1]

The two quotes that open this chapter are useful for grasping how the New Testament writers frame the meaning of their suffering in this context so rife with ordinary and extraordinary potential for hardship. The life of Jesus, complete with his ministries of teaching, preaching, and healing, provides both literally and figuratively new sight to the blind and new hope to the persecuted. The first quote is a story of Jesus healing the blind men, which is both a story of miraculous, physical healing and also a metaphor for the gift of new sight that people sought and received from Jesus. In response to their new sight, those who were touched by Jesus "follow." Their personal suffering is subsumed into the larger story of purpose and meaning of the life of Jesus, who heals and redeems their suffering. The second quote foretells that those who were touched by Jesus bore witness to (and even followed him into) mockery, scorn, abuse, and death. "But, after three days he will rise." It is, in a nutshell, the promise of rising after mockery, scorn, abuse, and death that summarizes the New Testament interpretation of suffering.

The New Testament writers are clear that suffering is suffering: real, painful, and unavoidable. But, suffering is not the last word for those who have hope. For, these Christians hope that like Jesus they will also rise again. This message was a powerful redefinition of suffering and hope for Gentiles and Jews living vulnerably under Roman occupation in a pre-modern era. And, it is this overarching message that the writers of the New Testament meant to convey. In order to explore more fully how the Christian writers came to this hopeful redefinition, it is useful to look closely at the writings themselves as categorized by their three main genres: gospels, letters, and apocalypse.

## Gospels

The gospels are a collection of four books that tell about the life, sayings, death, and Resurrection of Jesus. These books are titled Matthew, Mark, Luke, and John. They bear the names of persons to whom the authorship of the books has been historically attributed, although it is a matter of scholarly debate as to who actually wrote these texts. They are commonly dated in the following way: Mark (60 CE), Matthew (70–80 CE), Luke (70–80 CE), and John (90–110 CE). It is unlikely that any of the gospel writers actually knew Jesus (4 BCE–30 CE) in person during his lifetime.[2]

The word *gospel* means "good news," and gives insight into the content of these books. While they tell the story of the life of Jesus, they are not biographies in the modern sense. They omit many of the details about Jesus' life that a person today might want to know, such as: how he lived as a child, what he studied, what his parents were like, with whom did he play, whether he loved anyone intimately, what his personality was like, what he looked like, and so on. In addition to a paucity of information about the details of his life, the books also treat historical data somewhat loosely. A biographer today would (hopefully) carefully research dates, locations, the accuracy of stories people remembered about the subject, and so on. Ancient writers, however, took a different angle. They would compose "biographies" not as a close and objective study of someone's life but rather as a record of a notable person's outstanding achievements. As such, all the stories and details included in the ancient biography would be intended to highlight the heroic deeds and character of the person the work was celebrating. Like other ancient biographies, the gospel writers selectively use stories and information to confirm (rather than *to investigate*) their unique points of view about the meaning of Jesus' life and work. In each case, the writers felt they had very good news to share with the people reading their words.

Each gospel presents a slightly varied picture of Jesus, thereby revealing that each was written for a specific audience.[3] Of course, as the gospels were actually being composed, the writers themselves did not have the benefit of the whole, completed Bible (they were the ones writing it, after all!). So, they worked within their limited contexts, speaking to their own specific audiences. There were many "gospels" written in the first several hundred years of the Christian era,[4] but only four were chosen by the developing Christian community to be included in the canon of the Bible. The four Gospels taken together comprise a picture of how the majority of Christians by the second and third centuries understood Jesus. The major features of this portrait, illustrated below, reveal not only how the community understood Jesus but also how they understood suffering in light of Jesus:

- *Jesus the miracle worker*. In all of the Gospels, Jesus is portrayed as a figure who produces miracles on behalf of the needy or the sick. The miracles have different meanings for the Gospel writers. For example, in the Gospel of Mark, Jesus produces miracles, but he instructs his disciples to keep his deeds, and thereby his identity, a secret (for example, Mark 5:41–43). By contrast in the Gospel of John, Jesus' miracles are called "signs," and Jesus performs them for the specific purpose of revealing his identity (for example, John 11:11–25). In both cases, nevertheless, the tradition records Jesus as doing miraculous things for the people who suffer physical ailments (blindness, leprosy, bleeding, and so on), bereavement, and varied forms of social and religious stigmatization. The miracles of Jesus as recorded in the New Testament were a source of inspiration and hope for suffering Christians of the earliest days of the religion, as they have continued to be until the present day.

- *Jesus the suffering servant.* The Gospels present the suffering of Jesus in various ways, but all are clear about the fact that he suffered in his life. The infancy narratives of Jesus' birth in the Gospels of Luke (2:1–7) and Matthew (1:18–24) portray Jesus' birth as humble and at risk. Matthew's gospel, further, tells a tale of persecution, as the infant's parents have to flee to Egypt to protect their son from state capture and murder (2:13–19). Mark's Gospel portrays Jesus as profoundly misunderstood by his family and his disciples, even when he tells them plainly who he is (for example, see 3:31–34 and 9:30–32). The Gospels of Mark, Luke, and Matthew together portray Jesus as betrayed by an intimate, denied and abandoned by his closest friends in his greatest hour of need, and ultimately tortured to death (see the conclusion of the Gospels beginning with Mark 14; Luke 22; and Matthew 26). In Mark, Jesus' final words are a woeful expression of abandonment, as Jesus cries out, "My God, my God, why have you forsaken me?" (15:34).
- *Jesus the Messiah/Christ.* Drawing on the ancestral hope of the Hebrew people for a king-deliverer from occupation and persecution, the Gospel writers portray Jesus as the anointed one (in Hebrew *Messiah*, in Greek *Christos*). From the time of Babylonian captivity (586–539 BCE) onward, the Hebrews anticipated deliverance and restoration as a people (see the prophetic works of Jeremiah and Ezekiel, for example). Varied ideas circulated about how or when that would occur, and different sects of Judaism (Sadducees, Pharisees, Zealots, Essenes) sprang up around different forms of hope for deliverance. Not all Jews in the first century agreed that Jesus was the longed-for Messiah, especially because suffering and dying were not historically part of the job description of the Messiah. Moreover, for Jews believing that the Messiah would bring political change, Jesus could not have been the Messiah because he did not effect any political change or liberation for the Jewish people. However, for the Jewish followers of the first-century Jesus movement, Jesus *did* fulfill the criteria of the Messiah. They built a case that Jesus was foretold in the words of the prophets (such as in Isaiah 7:14), in the suffering of the prophets themselves (as in Jeremiah 12), in the customary practices of sacrifice and yearly atonement (as in Leviticus 16), and in the historical experience of a king suffering on behalf of his people (see the stories of Saul and David in 1 and 2 Samuel). Especially for the Jewish-influenced gospel writers such as Mark and Matthew, Jesus clarified once and for all that the Messiah had to suffer and die for his people in order to bring about their deliverance. Jesus' suffering and dying, they argued, are not God's rejection of Jesus but rather God's intent for Jesus as the Messiah.

- *Jesus the redeemer.* Were the intent for Jesus' suffering to be the end of the story, the Gospels would not be very good news at all. The whole narrative of his life, however, comes to make sense in light of the Gospel claim of Jesus' Resurrection, that is, that three days after his death Jesus rose from the dead. It is sometimes helpful to note that this aspect of the story (along with the other miracles that Jesus is said to have performed) cannot be verified from a historical point of view. Yet, the claim that Jesus was risen is proof of the powerful conviction held by the Gospel writers themselves (and by their intended audiences) about Jesus' ultimate response to suffering. Although Jesus lived a human life fraught with loneliness, suffering, and a humiliating, painful death, they claimed he was yet victorious over it. As the one who is risen, the meaning of the Messiah as deliverer was now understood in a new light. The Messiah will not be a king of this world (as one perhaps might have been anticipating); rather, he will be a king of the cosmos and the one who ushers in what Matthew calls "the Kingdom of Heaven." The Gospels' purpose then is primarily to tell this *good news.*
- *Jesus the savior of the world.* The good news of the Gospels is extended beyond the life of Jesus in the book called Acts of the Apostles. This book is actually the second half of the Gospel of Luke. It extends the Jesus narrative into the origins of the first Christian community and tells how Jesus' teachings, life, death, and Resurrection traveled beyond Judah. The book details the actions of the apostles (people specially tasked to spread the message of Jesus) as they missionized and formed communities throughout the Roman Empire, eventually making it all the way to the heart of the Empire in Rome. In Acts, the reader learns of tremendous challenges the first Christians faced both internally and externally. A poignant example is the martyrdom of Stephen in Acts 7, in which the writer attributes to Stephen a long speech detailing the historic sins of Israel and the conflict between the religious establishment and the budding Christian community. The story concludes with the stoning of Stephen and the Christian men and women being dragged off to prison. The stories of martyrdom and imprisonment in Acts are matched with heroic tales of faith, conversions, and miracles. Acts concludes with the apostle Paul's arrival in Rome, where he preaches Jesus and his message about the Kingdom of God without hindrance. The achievement of Acts is the continuation of Jesus' story into the life of the Christian community. The events and life of Jesus here become attached to the struggle of the nascent church, and Jesus' suffering becomes attached to the promise of salvation for the whole world.

The Gospels and Acts do not present a formal theological study of the life of Jesus. Even more so, they do not present a tidy theology of suffering and dying. However, they do successfully establish the framework within which a formal Christian theology and, specifically, a theology of suffering can be developed. This framework involves the twin aspects of: 1) Jesus' ministry, life, death, and

Resurrection; and 2) the effect of this life on the community of his believers (i.e., the church). The integrative nature of the suffering, dying, and Resurrection of Jesus is presented as a single event – an event that has cosmic significance for the suffering and redemption of his followers. The effect of this event on the developing community is more explicitly considered in the letters of the New Testament.

## Letters

There are twenty-one books of the New Testament that are considered letters or epistles. In the ancient world, absent the conveniences of modern technologies and tools for communication and travel, epistles were the most frequent method people used to stay in touch with one another, especially when they were separated by great distances. The early Christians were widely scattered across the major cities of the Roman Empire. Missionaries such as the apostle Paul used letters as a means of introducing themselves to people they intended to visit as well as to stay in touch with communities they had already established.

The letters are divided into groups. The "Pauline letters" are generally believed to have been authored authentically by the apostle Paul and include 1 Thessalonians, 1 Corinthians, 2 Corinthians, Philippians, Philemon, Galatians, and Romans. These seven letters consist of Paul's correspondence to the church communities in each of these cities. Three additional letters, called the "deutero-Pauline letters," are attributed to Paul but were probably not written by him: Ephesians, Colossians, and 2 Thessalonians. The "pastoral letters," addressed to pastors of the churches in the cities bearing their names, are 1 Timothy, 2 Timothy, and Titus. These letters are also attributed to Paul, although the authenticity of Paul's authorship is disputed. The remaining seven letters, called the "catholic epistles," are written for a universal (*catholic* means universal) audience. With the exception of the Letter to the Hebrews, the letters are named after a disciple: James, 1 Peter, 2 Peter, 1 John, 2 John, 3 John, and Jude. All the letters were composed between roughly 50 and 120 CE, representing both the earliest and latest writings of the New Testament.

Like the Gospels, the letters do not represent a formal theology. They are largely situational, written to address specific situations or contexts of the communities for whom they were intended. The authors' goal in the letters is, generally, to provide guidance or instruction on right leadership, belief, and conduct for those who believe in Jesus. As such, the letters demonstrate a burgeoning theological effort at working out the way in which belief in Jesus as Messiah, redeemer, Son of Man, and so on, both applies to and reshapes the lifestyles, faith, and morals of the budding Christian community. The question of suffering, then, may be considered twofold: 1) in light of the developmental theologies of the letters; as well as 2) the experience of suffering of the communities for whom the developmental theologies were being written.[5] Considering some examples will help: 1 Thessalonians, Romans, 1 Peter, and Hebrews.

Biblical scholars generally agree that 1 Thessalonians is the first letter Paul wrote (that is, among those in the Bible), dating from around 50 CE. The letter is addressed to the Christian community in Thessalonica, where many people were apparently grieving over the death of some of their members. Paul's missionary activities had led him away from Thessalonica, but he stayed in touch through his companion Timothy. Timothy reported to Paul on the condition of the Thessalonian church, prompting this letter in which Paul is tasked to praise the community's faith, to solidify his own good standing as a missionary among them, and to deal with their morals and beliefs. After a customary greeting and statement of thanksgiving for the good faith of the people of Thessalonica, Paul fills his audience in on his own recent travels and activities (2:17–3:8). Paul has to defend himself and his readers against "imitators of the churches of God" (2:14), namely, people who have challenged Paul's apostolic authority and teaching. One glimpses here the tension and contest over leadership of the churches in the first decades after Jesus.

In chapter 4, Paul addresses specifically the community's issues, such as sexual mores (4:3–8), charitable conduct (4:9–12), and church order (5:12–22). In 4:13–15:11, Paul deals with the community's question over why some of their loved ones have suffered and died. The context of the letter suggests that some of the community were expecting Jesus' return and are losing faith because their members are dying and Jesus has not yet come back. Paul's response to their question is to argue that earthly death is like sleep. It is not a permanent condition of loss but rather a temporary state in which both the living and the dead anticipate the return of Jesus. Paul frames present death in terms of ultimate hope for resurrection, just as Jesus rose, even though the living cannot know the timeframe for when this will happen. The dead and the living, in Jesus, will always be together, and thus believers should not grieve hopelessly. This argument is encapsulated in the following passage (4:13–18):

> We do not want you to be unaware, brothers, about those who have fallen asleep, so that you may not grieve like the rest, who have no hope. For if we believe that Jesus died and rose, so too will God, through Jesus, bring with him those who have fallen asleep. Indeed, we tell you this, on the word of the Lord, that we who are alive, who are left until the coming of the Lord, will surely not precede those who have fallen asleep. For the Lord himself, with a word, a command, with the voice of an archangel and with the trumpet of God, will come down from heaven, and the dead in Christ will rise first. Then, we who are alive, who are left, will be caught up together with them in the clouds to meet the Lord in the air. Thus, we shall always be with the Lord. Therefore, console one another with these words.

The Letter to the Romans is the longest and most theologically developed letter in the New Testament. It is a later work of Paul, dating to around 58 CE. Paul did not establish the church in Rome, so he writes this letter as a way of introducing himself. He states that he plans to visit the church, and he hopes to raise money from the Roman Christians to fund his missionary trip to Spain. As he attempts to garner a good reception as well as financial support, Paul offers the most systematic and formal presentation of his ideas in this letter. The letter begins with the typical address and proceeds to articulate Paul's understanding of the Christian faith: humanity lost to sin; justification through faith in Jesus; justification in Christian life; the relationship of Jews to Christians in God's overarching plan for salvation; and finally the responsibilities of Christian people. Paul does not offer details of Jesus' life (Paul did not actually know Jesus during Jesus' life). However, Paul does provide an understanding of the meaning of Jesus' suffering, dying, and Resurrection for Christians (and for the world at large) that becomes critical for the entire Christian tradition's thinking on the matter.

In Romans 3, Paul argues that human beings are universally in bondage to sin. The Old Testament law, according to Paul, did not help people to correct their bondage to sin; it merely pointed out to them how sinful they in fact were. Therefore, Paul proceeds to argue that the law itself cannot justify people, only faith in Christ. For Paul, forgiveness from sin is made possible by Jesus' bloodshed, and that forgiveness is given to those who have faith in Jesus. Of this, Paul says (3:24–26):

> They are justified freely by his grace through the redemption in Christ Jesus, whom God set forth as an expiation, through faith, by his blood, to prove his righteousness because of the forgiveness of sins previously committed, through the forbearance of God – to prove his righteousness in the present time, that he might be righteous and justify the one who has faith in Jesus.

Paul continues that Christian life is justified life, and through their baptism into the Christian faith people will be as adopted children of God. Because they have become children of God, they are then destined for the same resurrection as Jesus. The sufferings of the present age are nothing, according to Paul, because redemption and resurrection are the Christian's destiny (8:18–26).

The basic belief in redemptive suffering expressed in Paul's Letter to the Romans is concretely tested in the experiences of the intended communities reading The First Letter of Peter. This letter (there also is a Second Letter of Peter) is attributed to Jesus' close apostle Peter, although scholars debate whether Peter himself actually wrote this letter. If Peter wrote it, it would have been composed in the early 60s CE; if someone else wrote it, it is likely to have been authored between 70 and 90 CE. The letter is addressed to the Christians in the five provinces in Asia Minor, and it emphasizes such themes as the blessed status of the church; the need for Christians to live moral and exemplary lives in the midst of non-Christians; and how to endure oppression. This letter's particular focus on the problem of the community's suffering sheds light on the historical context of its writing. The Christians of Asia Minor were being persecuted, and the letter instructs them to find purpose and hope in their suffering for God's name. Their suffering becomes a mark of the authenticity of their faith and an indicator of reward to come. Their suffering is furthermore likened to Jesus' own suffering, in which fleshly (bodily, earthly) suffering and death are contrasted with glorified, spiritual life. As Jesus' suffering demonstrated obedience to the will of God and led to the Resurrection, so too will the suffering of 1 Peter's audience become a path to glory:

> Now who is going to harm you if you are enthusiastic for what is good? But even if you should suffer because of righteousness, blessed are you. Do not be afraid or terrified with fear of them [i.e., those who persecute them], but sanctify Christ as Lord in your hearts. Always be ready to give an explanation to anyone who asks you for a reason for your hope, but do it with gentleness and reverence, keeping your conscience clear, so that when you are maligned, those who defame your good conduct in Christ may themselves be put to shame. For it is better to suffer for doing good, or that be the will of God, than for doing evil.
>
> For Christ also suffered sins once, the righteous for the sake of the unrighteous, that he might lead you to God. Put to death in the flesh, he was brought to life in the spirit.
>
> (3:13–19)

> Therefore since Christ suffered in the flesh, arm yourselves also with the same attitude (for whoever suffers in the flesh has broken with sin), so as not to spend what remains of one's life in the flesh on human desires, but on the will of God.
>
> (4:1–2)

The Letter to the Hebrews is different from the other letters of the New Testament insofar as it blends aspects of letter writing within a generally more structured theological treatise. The text is probably from the early 100s CE, and the authorship is unknown (although tradition attributed the letter to Paul). The principal image in the letter is the Jerusalem Temple, and the author's purpose is to interpret Jesus' suffering and dying through the lens of the Temple's priesthood, worship practices, and animal sacrifice. Jesus is depicted as both the highest priest and also the perfect sacrifice, which fulfills the Old Testament law and brings about a new covenant between God and Christians. This letter's articulation of a theology of Jesus' sacrificial death would become a standard model for interpreting his suffering throughout the entire Christian tradition:

> But when Christ came as high priest of the good things that have come to be, passing through the greater and more perfect tabernacle not made by hands, that is, not belonging to this creation, he entered once and for all into the sanctuary, not with the blood of goats and calves but with his own

> blood, thus obtaining eternal redemption. For if the blood of goats and bulls and the sprinkling of heifer's ashes can sanctify those who are defiled so that their flesh is cleansed, how much more will the blood of Christ, who through the eternal spirit offered himself unblemished to God, cleanse our conscience from dead works to worship the living God. For this reason he is the mediator of a new covenant.
>
> (9:11–12)

When considered together, the New Testament letters provide a vital picture of the birth of the Christian religion as it emerged in the discreet contexts of specific church communities throughout the Roman Empire. Although their specific circumstances differed one from another, eliciting a range of epistolary topics, they shared the common thread of attempting to live a new way of life. Misunderstood and often persecuted, the first Christian churches were no strangers to suffering. As expressed in the New Testament letters, the courage to remain steadfast in their beliefs was bolstered by the theological effort to understand their own suffering in light of Jesus' life, death, and Resurrection.

## Apocalypse – the Book of Revelation

The Book of Revelation is the final book of the Bible. The prologue of the book states that the revelation of Jesus Christ was made to the "servant John," through an angelic messenger. Early Christian tradition attributed authorship of the Book of Revelation to the same person who authored the Gospel of John. It is unlikely, however, that the author is the same person. Most Bible scholars believe that the book was composed by a prophet (or at least a person writing in the Hebraic prophetic tradition) toward the end of the first century CE. In this era, the Roman Emperor Domitian reigned (81–96 CE), and his rule was characterized by brutal persecution of Christians.[6] The context of the writing, therefore, is one of intense suffering and vulnerability. This context shapes the literary genre of this book, which is called "apocalyptic."

"Apocalyptic" literature derives its name from the term *apocalypse*, which means "revelation." The revelations in works of apocalyptic tend to be highly symbolic descriptions of visions and voices, which are communicated to a human recorder through a divine medium (such as an angel). Apocalyptic literature was a popular form of writing from the third century BCE until the second century BCE. This type of writing was (and is) particularly appealing to people under duress because it provides a stylistically cryptic way of simultaneously voicing and disguising opposition to political oppression.

In this particular book, the revelations include both visions and voices that come to John through an angel during his time in exile on the island of Patmos (he has been exiled for proclaiming his Christian beliefs). All of John's visions are filled with important symbolism, so that the images themselves cannot be taken literally or at face value, as is the case with all apocalyptic literature. The images mean and bear reference to more than the actual things John depicts.

For example, in chapter four, John records a vision of heavenly worship. In the image, he describes a dazzling heavenly throne, surrounded by twenty-four elders in white garments and wearing golden crowns. He further describes the throne surrounded by four living creatures covered with eyes in front and in back, inside and out. The four creatures are a lion, an ox, a human being, and an eagle. Each creature has six wings (4:6–8). At face value, the images convey an impressive heavenly court. Symbolically, however, they mean much more. There are twenty-four elders, which is two times twelve. Twelve means perfect wholeness, as it stands for the twelve tribes of Israel. The elders are wearing white and gold, colors that represent triumph. There are four beasts, representing the world in its four corners, and each is permeated with eyes, representing total sight and knowledge. Their six wings are a reference to the seraphim from the heavenly court described in the prophet Isaiah 6:2. The animals respectively represent nobility (lion), strength (ox), wisdom (humanity), and speed (eagle). In their full symbolism, the heavenly court represents the perfection of God's rule, the totality of God's wisdom, and the power and dignity of God's creation.[7]

In the context of Domitian's persecution, the Book of Revelation is for the author a symbolic way of denouncing and resisting the persecution the Christians faced, while at the same time encouraging them to remain steadfast in their faith no matter what they might endure. As such, in the book's opening visions, John writes letters to seven churches of Asia, in which he shares awesome images and exhortations pertinent to each of their local situations. These exhortations are encouragements to the churches to remain strong during their trials. He follows with his account of the heavenly court and a scroll bound by seven seals. As the seals are broken, the violence, plagues, famine, and death that will befall the churches are revealed. Communicated in symbolic imagery, this violence represents the reality of the religious persecution the communities are actually enduring. John interrupts the violence with a victorious vision of the redemption of the twelve tribes of Israel (multiplied by thousands), who numerically represent scores of people too great to count. Then, John continues with the terrifying story of the woman giving birth to the Son of Man (Jesus), pursued and hunted by the great Dragon, followed by celestial warfare between God and Satan. The Dragon is depicted as being expelled from heaven to earth, where he relentlessly pursues the mother and the rest of her offspring (who represent the church). Then, emerge the beast (the antichrist who is anti- or against Christians) and the Harlot of Babylon (namely, Rome). The book concludes with the downfall of Babylon, the victory of God, the redemption of the persecuted, and the glorious New Jerusalem for the Christian faithful.

The entire Book of Revelation may be considered a treatise on why God permits the suffering of the church under persecution. The book seems to answer that God allows the suffering and persecution of his people, and yet that suffering is to be accepted because it is temporal. It is ultimately to be met with peace and the final perfection of God's reign. The theology in the book must accommodate and account for the fact that it is Christians who are suffering.

The author reasons that their suffering must all somehow fit into God's plan. The thrust of the revelations, then, becomes how to endure suffering appropriately and to find hope in its midst. The following passage captures Revelation's sentiment of questioning, hope, and the struggle to endure (6:9–11):

> When he broke open the fifth seal, I saw underneath the souls of those who had been slaughtered because of the witness they bore to the word of God. They cried out in a loud voice, "How long will it be, holy and true master, before you sit in judgment and avenge our blood on the inhabitants of the earth?" Each of them was given a white robe, and they were told to be patient a little while longer until the number was filled of their fellow servants and brothers who were going to be killed as they had been.

The hope for judgment and vindication that this passage alludes to is not immediately met. The death continues, and suffering carries on. The real hope of the revelations must become *eschatological*. Eschatological is a theological term that means "study of the future." It refers to things in their ultimate or final sense. Eschatological hope in the Book of Revelation is hope for a good and just resolution to all life for all of creation; to a final victory of goodness over evil forces; and a lasting reign of peace instead of violence and warfare. These things cannot be realized in life for the suffering Christians (of the first century or of any century), so regular hope gives way to a final hope. For John, this hope is attached to and seen through his belief in Jesus' Resurrection. A glorious vision of what the oppressed can hope for is expressed in the final chapter of the Book of Revelation (22:1–5):

> Then the angel showed me the river of life-giving water, sparkling like crystal, flowing from the throne of God and the Lamb [i.e., Christ] down the middle of its street. On either side of the river grew the tree of life that produces fruit twelve times a year, once each month; the leaves of the trees serve as medicine for the nations. Nothing accursed will be found there anymore. The throne of God and the Lamb will be in it, and his servant will worship him. They will look upon his face, and his name will be on their foreheads. Night will be no more, nor will they need light from lamp or sun, for the Lord God shall give them light, and they shall reign forever and ever.

## Conclusion

The New Testament places the experience of human suffering in the framework of the life of Jesus. The principal message of the New Testament, whether one is reading the gospels, the letters, or revelations, is one of hope. Like the books of the Old Testament, the New Testament does not gloss over the experience of suffering. To the contrary, suffering is depicted in sometimes agonizing detail. Perhaps the most poignant example of this is the suffering of Jesus himself. That Jesus really suffered is in part how Christians can be comforted in their own suffering. Through Jesus' experience, God knows what they themselves are going through. Even more, God as Father is depicted in places as party to suffering, as for example in the oft-quoted passage John 3:16: "For God so loved the world that he gave his only Son, so that everyone who believes in him might not perish but have eternal life."

Again, as with the Old Testament writings, questions about suffering can still be asked, "Why would God allow this situation in the first place?" "Could God not have come up with a better plan than this?" The New Testament writings do not directly tackle these questions. In fact, the experience of Jesus' suffering, and human suffering at large, juxtaposed with the belief in God's total goodness and justice, is largely what gives rise to the problem of suffering. Why would God solve the problems of the world by sacrificing Jesus? How does such a death actually save people? And so on. What the New Testament does do, however, is provide an answer for Christians to the question over how God responds to suffering. The New Testament answer is: Jesus' Resurrection. Suffering and death are met *eschatologically* by resurrection and eternal life with God. Jesus' Resurrection becomes a window into a universal, future possibility of new life. Hope for this possibility is so great for the New Testament writers that it enables them to endure suffering and persecution, to pray for their tormentors, and to encourage one another in the face of circumstances that would otherwise lead to despair. The questions that this basic hope leaves unanswered, then, become the material for later generations of Christian theologians. It is to the theological endeavor to answer how Jesus' suffering and dying might save others that we now turn.

## Questions for review and discussion

1. What are the three main types of literature in the New Testament? How might you characterize the discussion of suffering in each?
2. Describe the communal nature of suffering among the first Christians. How does this suffering connect to Jesus' suffering?
3. What modern-day examples of religious persecution can you think of? What encourages people to maintain faith in the midst of suffering?
4. Describe the hope of the New Testament writers. Do you find it persuasive?

## Resources

Bauckman, Richard. *The Theology of the Book of Revelation*. Cambridge and New York: Cambridge University Press, 1993.

Brown, Raymond E., Joseph A. Fitzmeyer, and Roland E. Murphy, Eds. *The New Jerome Bible Commentary*. London: Geoffrey Chapman, 1996.

Matera, Frank J. *New Testament Christology*. Louisville, Kentucky: Westminster John Knox Press, 1999.

Tambasco, Anthony J., Ed. *The Bible on Suffering: Social and Political Implications*. New York: Paulist Press, 2002.

*Saint Mary's Press College Study Bible*. Winona, Minnesota: Saint Mary's Press, 2007.

# 4 Soteriology, Part I

## Historical interpretations of the meaning and efficacy of the Cross

[It] should not surprise us that, when an innocent man was viewed as yielding up his life freely, he should have been seen as an offering for sin. That Israel repudiated human sacrifice should not have posed a barrier. The whole Jewish culture was familiar with animal victims symbolic of the repentant human spirit. It was a short step from there to seeing in this sinless human victim Jesus as an expiatory sin offering.

Gerard S. Sloyan[1]

### Introduction

In Christian theology, the term "soteriology" refers to the study of the soter or savior. Specifically, it is the study of Jesus as the savior. The major question involved in this area of theology is: *how may Jesus be understood as humanity's savior?* Does his life save people? Do his suffering and death save people? Does his Resurrection save? How and in what way? By what mechanism does this one person's death effect salvation for others? Moreover, what *is* salvation? What are people saved from, and when are they saved?

The questions of soteriology lie at the heart of Christian faith. However, despite the centrality of the belief that Jesus' death is salvific, the Christian community throughout the ages has not always maintained a standard way of answering the questions of soteriology. Variations in the community's understanding of Jesus' death over the past two millennia reflect the process by which all theology develops. The conventions and situations of any era constitute the backdrop of life, and people of every era think about religious faith in modes current with their own contemporary worldviews. Christians have thus engaged in a process of understanding Jesus' life and death in ways appropriate to their own circumstances. This is not to say that the theological tradition wildly varies from one age to the next, but it is to emphasize that all aspects of theology, including soteriology, require people's "buy-in" if the theological claims are actually going to be persuasive and comforting in one's own context.

Salvation, in particular, requires people's "buy-in," in part because the circumstances in which people live and die can so dramatically differ from one context (geographical and temporal) to the next. Imagine all the differences, for example, between life in twenty-first century America and life in first-century Palestine. Yet, Christians in both contexts were/are challenged to make sense of their own life's experiences vis-à-vis their belief in Jesus. A historical-developmental approach that looks at belief as it emerges and changes over time, therefore, is best in considering the question of how Jesus' suffering, life and death are salvific in Christian theology. While the following chapter will consider more contemporary approaches, this chapter considers the following major historical periods: biblical foundations, the patristic era, the Middle Ages/Renaissance, and the Reformation.

## Biblical foundations for soteriology

The roots for thinking about Jesus as a savior can be traced back to the eighth-century-BCE prophets who began the process of translating the doctrines of the tribal religion of Israel into a religion of ethical demand. These prophets witnessed the moral and religious failings of the Kingdom of Israel, and prophesied destruction because it had fallen away from the ethical precepts of Israel's covenant with God. The prophets trusted that a remnant of the people would be spared, from whom would rise a restored nation, and this belief generated a distinction between ethnic Israel (or Israel as a kingdom) and true Israel (or Israel as a people who carried the covenant in their hearts).

Over the centuries of foreign occupation, Israel's national hopes for a restored kingdom remained unfulfilled. As their oppression became greater under increasingly powerful world empires, the prophetic hope for a new kingdom gave way to an apocalyptic hope for an entirely new world (see Ezekiel 37, for example). Many came to see this present world as characterized by extreme alienation, and one from which God's sovereignty had apparently fled. Only those who stayed on the side of righteousness would be redeemed in an ultimate sense (see, for example, 2 Maccabees 7:9).

With the shift toward personal moral responsibility (as opposed to communal moral responsibility) that characterized Israel's prophets during and after the Babylonian Exile, one finds fracturing among how Israelites described what it meant to be "Israel." For some, personal conversion and bearing the covenant in one's heart, regardless of ethnic heritage, were most important (see the story of Ruth, for example); for others, it was having status as a descendant of the original tribal community (see Ezra and Nehemiah, for example). Many became intensely apocalyptic and they saw themselves as living in the last days, awaiting a Messiah who would inaugurate a new reign (such as the community of Essenes, known for their "Dead Sea Scrolls"). Others awaited an earthly regime change.

As an apocalyptic sect of Judaism, the first Christians believed that their Messiah had come.[2] It is important to understand, however, that after the death of Jesus, the developing church had to argue the case that Jesus was the Messiah. This involved a Christian soteriological exegesis (or interpretation) of Hebrew texts that stood in opposition to the traditional interpretations of the Hebrew scholars. This proved to be a tense and divisive task for the first Christians because Jesus' death on the Cross was so scandalous and difficult to explain.[3] For although there was the tradition of suffering in the Hebrew literature, there was no element in the tradition that openly anticipated a dying Messiah.

If it were not for the Resurrection experience, Jesus' disciples would likely have let the movement end. It was conviction of this powerful belief, namely, that Jesus was risen, that led the disciples to reassemble in Jerusalem (they had fled at Jesus' death) and try to understand the experience. The disciples concluded that a miracle had indeed happened in Jesus' rising from the dead, and that the final advent of the Kingdom of God had not been put off by this death. To the contrary, Jesus' death had ushered it in. Proclaiming faith in Jesus became the necessary condition for the Kingdom's arrival. Moreover, those who proclaimed this message identified themselves with the remnant of Israel, foretold by the prophets, that would be saved. These Jewish Christians still had to connect this belief with the scriptures, so they established an interpretation to make sense of their claims about Jesus that connected their beliefs with the ancient prophecies. They found evidence in such places as the suffering servant of Isaiah (42–53); the Psalms; Daniel 7 in which the Son of Man reappears with God in glory at the Judgment; and others.[4]

The Christians connected all these ideas and linked them to one identity – namely Jesus. They developed the soteriology of Jesus as the Prophet-King-Son-of-Man of whom it was written that he must suffer, be rejected, and be killed in order to rise again on the third day and to be returned to heaven until the time that he would be revealed in glory at the right hand of God at the advent of the Kingdom.

Those who believed in this interpretation of scripture, repented of their sins, and believed in the name of Jesus, would inherit the promises God made to the people of Israel. Salvation could be found through the name of Jesus alone. Jesus' life came to be seen as the ideal servanthood, perfecting the previous works of the prophets (such as Moses), the priests (such as Aaron), and the kings (such as David). Jesus came to be seen, further, as the ultimate surrogate sacrifice, restoring the covenant between God and humanity perfectly, in contrast to the imperfect and oft-repeated animal sacrifices.

In temple worship animals were sacrificed as sin and guilt offerings; on feast days; on Passover; and on the annual Day of Atonement. At Yom Kippur, the Day of Atonement, Israel would atone for the sins of the year to come through: 1) the ritual penance of the high priest; and 2) the priest's laying his hands upon the head of a scapegoat who would be driven into the wilderness to die. This action was undertaken to cleanse Israel, and especially the temple sanctuary, of collective sin and religious irregularities that would defile people for communion with God. The laying on of hands was an act of transferring the sin onto the sacrificial goat (Lev. 16:1–34). Christians interpreted Jesus' death in this same light. In his Crucifixion, they understood Jesus (like the scapegoat) to be the one onto whom were transferred the sins of humanity. Jesus' sacrificial death erased humanity's sins once and for all.

In this light, Christians used terms such as "ransom" to express how Jesus' sacrificial death effected human salvation (for example, Mark 10:45/Matthew 20:28 – "For the Son of Man himself came not to be served but to serve, and to give his life as a ransom for many"). They described his bloodshed as binding a new covenant with God (for example, Mark 14:22–25/Matthew 26:26–29/Luke 22:19–20 – "This is my blood, the blood of the covenant, poured out for many"). Paul offers a variety of ideas to explain how Jesus' death effects salvation. Paul offered that Jesus acts as a vicarious substitution in a sin offering (2 Cor 5:21); that Jesus' death reconciles people to God (2 Cor 5:19); and that Jesus' death initiates a new creation (2 Cor 5:16–17). In short, the earliest Christians argued that Jesus' sacrifice justified believers and enabled them to become adopted children of God.

In summarizing the New Testament perspective, one might say that the foundations for soteriology represent a Christian reading of the Hebrew tradition. Largely informed by the early Jewish Christian worldview, the Christians established a basic message of universal salvation, lived out in community, and accessed individually through faith in Jesus. The saving work of the Cross was understood to be one half of the equation; the other was the human response in faith to Jesus. God the Father and Jesus were depicted as subjects of the Cross, and Jesus' sacrifice was described as freely offered. The fine-tuning of this basic model continued in the subsequent eras.

## Patristic soteriology

The patristic era, named after the Latin word *pater* meaning "father," is the period between the second and seventh centuries. This period witnessed the transition from Jewish Christianity into a largely Gentile (or non-Jewish) movement. The period also witnessed the infant Church becoming acclimated to the broader Greco-Roman culture. In the first two hundred years of the patristic era, Christians suffered cruel and violent persecution by Roman authorities. Only after Emperor Constantine converted to Christianity in the early fourth century did the persecutions end.[5]

Over this period great debates arose about the nature of God and Christ. These debates were fueled by the fact that large distances separated Christians in the East from those in the West (often causing rivalries); Christians frequently spoke either Latin or Greek but not both; and Christians came from a variety of cultural heritages that shaped how they thought theologically. For example, Jewish Christians were predisposed to think about God as a simple monotheism (one God), while Gentile Christians were predisposed to thinking about God as a plural (such as in the polytheistic model of the Greek and Roman pantheons). These backgrounds affected how Christians understood the nature and relationship between God the Father, God the Son, and God the Holy Spirit.

With its new imperial status under Constantine in the fourth century, Christianity was tasked to end its debates and clarify its core beliefs. As a result, throughout the patristic era, Christians met in synods and councils in order to define orthodox (correct) doctrine over and against beliefs deemed heretical. Although they turned to the New Testament for help, patristic era Christians did not discover an unambiguous account of the mystery of the One whom they proclaimed as the Christ. They found several biblical titles for Jesus: Christ, Logos, Son of God, Son of Man. And, each of the titles expressed a unique relationship between Jesus and God, but they did not conclusively express what the specific nature of that relationship was. Developing an "orthodox" understanding of the Trinity (i.e., the Christian belief that God is one and yet three persons of Father, Son, and Spirit) was therefore highly controversial. As the patristic era Christians struggled to arrive at orthodox language for describing this mystery, it became increasingly clear that the right theology depended on a proper understanding of the salvific efficacy of Jesus' death and Resurrection.

Efforts at developing a proper understanding of Christ (called "Christology") began early on.[6] For example, Justin Martyr, ca. 100–165, in his work called *First Apology*, argued that Jesus is properly understood as the *Logos*, or Word of God. Justin held that it is through God's Word that God creates (as in Genesis 1), and it is the Word that became *incarnated* in the person Jesus. In this way, Jesus may be rightly understood as God. Justin's Logos theology, however, subordinated the divinity of Jesus to that of the Father, making Jesus somehow lesser than God proper.

Irenaeus of Lyons, ca. 120–202, in his work *Against Heresies*, attempted to battle the Gnostic Christian claims that Jesus only *seemed* to be human. The Gnostics denied that Jesus was really a human being, which Irenaeus found highly problematic. For, he argued, if the human body of Jesus is rejected, or if Jesus did not entirely assume a human nature, the salvific power of Jesus' sacrificial death would be lost. If it only *seems* to be a body, it is not a very good substitutionary sacrifice. For Irenaeus, what happened to humanity in the fall of Adam was corrected (or *recapitulated*) in Jesus' authentic human life and death.

Other writers of the era included Tertullian and Origen. Tertullian, ca. 160–?, in his work *Against Praxeas*, developed the Trinitarian language of the one divine substance (*substantiae*) in three persons (*personae*) of the Trinity (*trinitas*), whose distinctions lie in their level or degree (*gradus*) within the divine hierarchy. And, Origen, ca. 185–254, in *On First Principles*, offered the first comprehensive, speculative, systematic theology of the age. Here he explored the idea of God as "the first principle." As there can only be one first principle, Origen argued, the Son cannot also be a first principle. Although the Son and the Spirit are divine, they are constituted by respectively lesser portions of divine substance than the Father.

All these writers struggled to find the right language for arguing that Jesus was really God and really human without falling into one of four errors: the first error was making Jesus so much the same as God that there was no distinction between the two, leading to the conclusion that God the Father actually died on the Cross; the second error was so much separating Jesus and God that one must conclude they are actually two separate deities, like Zeus and Poseidon; the third error was arguing so stringently for the divinity of Jesus that his humanity became artificial, like a disguise or costume; and the fourth error was arguing so stringently for the humanity of Jesus that he became something other than true God, such as a special human-angelic creation or merely an adopted human son.[7]

Driving the patristic debates over the nature of Jesus and his relationship to God was the fundamental question of how Jesus' life and death were efficacious for human salvation. These writers believed Jesus *was* salvific, but they struggled to articulate *how* properly to understand and communicate that belief. In Walter H. Principe's survey of this process, he summarizes the following major themes and language that emerged from the patristic era's efforts at understanding Christ's saving work:[8]

1 The Father's economy or plan – the saving work on the Cross is God's Trinitarian life (Father-Son-Spirit) played out in the history of creation. The work is initiated and undertaken out of God's love and providential care for humanity.
2 The Incarnation is itself the saving work, whereby the second person of the Trinity (the Son, the Word) is incarnate in the life of Jesus and restores for all humanity what Adam lost. In taking on human life, Jesus restores and redeems human nature to friendship with God.
3 Christ the Teacher makes known a new way of life, and salvation is modeled in the good and obedient life of Jesus.
4 Christ's death and Resurrection are examples to imitate. Jesus both teaches what God is like and what is required of human beings, and he also establishes the way through his sacrificial death.
5 Christ's perfect obedience even unto death demonstrates a love of God and affects humanity by eliciting from people faith, hope, love, and sorrow.
6 Christ's work is a victory over sin, death, and the devil. Where human beings were enslaved to the devil through their sin, Christ pays the ransom with his death and liberates humanity to new life.

## Soteriology in the Middle Ages and Renaissance

The Middle Ages describes the period in Europe between roughly the eighth and thirteenth centuries. The term Renaissance describes the period in Europe between roughly the fourteenth and fifteenth centuries. During these eras, the Christian religion and churches underwent significant contextual events and developments that transformed the shape and legacy of the religious tradition. For example, toward the end of the patristic period, the Roman Empire fell to Germanic peoples conquering from the north. The establishment of these new monarchies ushered in the feudal system of medieval Europe. Landed nobles and monarchs often had vested interests in church leadership, and so their presence helped to shape (and sometimes contributed to the corruption of) the medieval church. As another example, in the seventh and eighth centuries, Islam began to spread, especially throughout Eastern Europe, leading eventually to the bloody legacy of the Crusades (fierce contests over land, political rule, and religious dominance). Other features of the age, such as the inventions of new technologies, the birth of trade guilds, and the devastating impact of the bubonic plague, affected daily life and the religious response to it.

Among the major church developments of this age were reform efforts initiated by key popes (such as Gregory VII in 1085); the widespread application of the Code of Canon Law; the schism between Eastern and Western Christianity (in 1054); and the establishment of monastic and secular universities. The circumstances of this era led to significant developments in Christian theology insofar as the faith needed to be stated in its most reasonable and persuasive form if it was to be a sound basis for law, if it was to retain its integrity in the face of the competing claims of Islam, and if it was to retain its integrity in the face of secular academic investigations. The result was the production of "scholastic" theology, which was a model of doing theology that attempted a comprehensive systematization of the whole system of beliefs in order to achieve an inherently reasonable and externally persuasive Christian worldview. The enthusiastic merging of reason and faith in this "scientific" approach to theology led theologians to close consideration and integration of biblical sources and the writings of the patristic tradition. If the patristic era was tasked with the formulation of doctrine, the Middle Ages was tasked with its refinement.

The approach to soteriological questions in this era, then, must be considered against this changing backdrop. Among the most salient features of this backdrop include: the goal of systematizing all religious doctrines into a cohesive whole; the feudal political system; and the overarching struggle of the era in which people suffered as a matter of course. The systematic goal meant for medieval theologians that they would need to make a fine argument for how Jesus' life and death were salvific that actively integrated doctrines of God, creation, sin, grace, and so on. The feudal backdrop meant that the values of station, rank, duty, honor, and satisfaction between serf and lord would inform the shape of their theological language. The hardships of the age meant that sin and suffering loomed large in the popular imagination.

J. Patout Burns' study[9] of soteriology in the Middle Ages, summarized below, provides a helpful tool for considering how major thinkers of this era incorporated these features into their thought on salvation. Anselm of Canterbury (1033–1109), for example, in his principal treatise on this subject called *Cur Deus Homo* (Why God Became Man), argued along the following lines. In dishonoring God through failure to submit to God's will, the human race of Adam incurred physical death and the loss of eternal happiness. This original loss ought to be restored by making satisfaction to God, which would include the twofold process of: 1) making up for the dishonor shown to God in the act of sinning; and 2) giving something dear and previously not required to God as a gesture of goodwill.

The problem for humanity was that human beings had no ability to make up for the gravity of offending God, nor had they anything precious to offer God. For, sin was not considered proportionate to the offense itself but proportionate to the one offended.[10] Hence, even the minutest sin against God was viewed as infinitely abhorrent and infinitely disfiguring to God's honor. God cannot simply forgive sin, Anselm argued, without incurring further dishonor by ignoring the demands of God's justice. Thus, in order to satisfy the obligation incurred by sin, humanity required one who *ought* to make up for the sin (i.e., a human being) as well as one who *could* make up for the sin (i.e., God). Hence, humanity needed the God-man.

According to Anselm, this God-man was Jesus. The death of Jesus satisfied the evil wrought by sin because it was a good that exceeded the previous obligations of man *and* it was proportionate to God's honor. Jesus, free from sin, was not obligated to die, and yet he willingly underwent death. His death should not be thought of as the penalty required by God but rather as the consequence of living perfectly in a sinful world – herein lies the good offering. Because Christ's death was meritorious, it warranted a reward, which Christ (as God) did not need. As such, Jesus transferred the merits of his death to his human followers as forgiveness for sins. According to Anselm, it is in this fashion that God's elect are restored to eternal life.

Anselm's basic model of satisfaction influenced all the medieval theologians on this question of soteriology, although some emphasized different elements in the nature and effect of the satisfaction. For example, Peter Abelard (1079–1142), in his *Commentary on the Romans*, argued that satisfaction for sin involves both: 1) eliminating contempt for God; and 2) enduring punishment for sin. Christ's death addresses both components of sin. On the one hand, the example of Christ's love and obedience can move human beings to eliminate contempt for God in their wills. Abelard thus stressed in particular the moral influence of Christ's work on correcting the human will, although this alone does not correct or alleviate the penalty of death. On the other hand, since Christ suffered corporeal death, which *was* the punishment due to God for human sin, it became possible for this penalty to be remitted as well.

Hugh of St. Victor (1096–1141), in his work *De Sacramentis*, also argued that the satisfaction for sin was won through the penalty of death being paid by an innocent victim. Hugh argued that God suffered the loss of man in the fall of Adam, and God also had to endure man's contempt. Since no descendant of Adam was innocent, no descendant of Adam could satisfy man's sin. Therefore, in God's mercy, God became man in order to make an offering of Himself as an innocent in order to meet God's own demand for justice, thereby restoring what was lost in Adam. The form the satisfaction took was Christ's punishment of corporeal death. The death of a sinner, while it would have been just punishment, would not have satisfied the penalty owed to God because death is merely a sinner's due. However, by an innocent man accepting the penalty of death (i.e., Jesus), the contempt originally shown to God by Adam was satisfied and mercy attained.

Peter Lombard (1100–1160), in his *Sentences*, adapted the theory of satisfaction to focus on the issue of humility and pride. Lombard argued there is not a penalty exacted per se; rather, humanity was restored to God through an act of humility that was greater than the act of pride demonstrated by Adam. In other words, satisfaction was wrought by the submission of insubordinate man to God. Thus, Lombard reasoned, Christ was more humiliated in his passion than Adam was proud in his disobedience. Humanity's relationship with God was opened to those who believe in Christ and subsequently undergo baptism and penance. Love of Christ alleviates the temptation to pride, and Jesus' "humility" remits humanity's eternal condemnation. Lombard's emphasis on humility was echoed and elaborated in Albert the Great's (1206–80) *Commentary on the Sentences*.

Thomas Aquinas (1225–74), an exemplar of scholastic theology, considered soteriology in both his *Summa Theologiae, tertia pars* and in his *Commentary on the Sentences*. Aquinas argued that human sin: 1) showed contempt for the infinite good; 2) turned from the infinite to the created order; and 3) lost the infinite to which it was destined. Christ's work therefore needed: 1) to make satisfaction for the offense against God; 2) to offer an equivalent to the good that was lost in the corruption of humanity through sin; and 3) to be capable of affecting and hence restoring all human beings. Aquinas argued that all this is accomplished in the following way. First, because Jesus was both divine and human, Christ's corporeal life is of greater value than the eternal lives of other humans. Thus, Jesus' death satisfies the penalty for both actual sins people commit and the original sin of Adam. Second, because Christ is both God and man, his offering is of infinite value and thus can restore the infinite corruption that was incurred under Adam. Finally, the divinity of Christ renders him powerful over all humanity, enabling him to communicate the merits of his work to the entire race of men. Thus, Aquinas held, Jesus' death has salvific power over all of humanity.

Among the others of this era, these theologians together offered a critical lens into the important themes of the age. Among them, one sees their heavy emphasis on humanity's sinfulness. The need to redress or pay for sin seemed to them essential if God's justice (as well as God's goodness or kindness) was to be kept intact. The scholastics, therefore, developed elaborate theological explanations that could accommodate the balance of God's mercy and God's demand for righteousness. Moreover, these thinkers wanted to understand the mechanism of how humanity might participate in salvation. To this end, these writers sought explanations for the function of the church in mediating or communicating Jesus' grace toward the end of humanity's forgiveness and restoration. The scholastic systems were big and complex, as they tried to comprehensively understand God in relationship to humanity vis-à-vis Jesus as the savior. It was precisely the complexity of the elaborate apparatus for receiving God's grace that reform-minded thinkers would reject in the era that followed.

## Soteriology in the Reformation

The term "Reformation" refers to the theological and institutional changes in the Christian churches of Western Europe during the sixteenth through eighteenth centuries. A number of factors led to the Reformation, including, but not limited to, corruption in the Roman Catholic Church leadership, economic impoverishment of the masses of people, greater popular literacy as an outcome of the Humanist movement, and (for the first time ever) the common availability of the Bible in print in the vernacular languages of Europe due to the invention of the printing press. These factors converged to produce several "reform" movements that included the rejection of the papal authority of the Roman church and the establishment of new autonomous, national churches throughout Europe.[11]

Key reformers of the era included Martin Luther (1482–1546), a German-born, Augustinian monk, who rejected the Roman church's practice of selling "indulgences," monetary donations made by a grateful penitent whose sins had been absolved. Luther saw in this practice an implicit message that people could purchase forgiveness for sins. Luther's critique on this point and on others was primarily theological, and he had no immediate intention of breaking from the authority of the Church. However, because he refused to recant his theological critiques, Luther was ultimately excommunicated (that is, separated from the Church by a papal decree). His cause was supported by German princes, who embraced the idea of a national church, free from allegiance and taxation to Rome, giving birth to Lutheranism.[12]

Other major reform efforts and churches occurred under the leadership of figures such as John Calvin and Henry VIII of England. Calvin (1509–64) was a second-generation reformer who recognized the need for a systematic approach to reformed theology. Calvin thus authored the *Institutes of the Christian Religion* (finished in 1559), in which he systematically detailed his understanding of God, humanity's need for redemption, Jesus' work as the mediator of that redemption, and the role of the church. Calvin attempted to live out an ideal Christian society in Geneva, Switzerland, where his theological ideas were rigorously put into practice.[13] Henry VIII, for his part, broke from the authority of Rome for more personally driven political reasons. In the hopes of producing a male heir with Anne Boleyn, Henry VIII petitioned Rome for an annulment of his marriage to Catherine of Aragon. Pope Clement VII, himself captive at the time of the petition, did not rule in favor of Henry's request. So, after a period of political and ecclesial machinations, Henry simply had Catherine banished, installed Anne Boleyn as queen, and declared himself head of the new Church of England. This began the reform church movement known as Anglicanism.[14]

As is clear from this brief mention of the era, theological concerns were not the only ones that influenced the shape of the Reformation. However, the climate of the day was ripe for institutional and theological updating. Beginning with the Humanist philosophers of the Renaissance, a new focus on individual human beings and their education began to spark interest in questions of personal spirituality and salvation. New access to the Bible, both because it was now available in the common language and inexpensively reproduced through new printing technology, opened up the religious imagination in a way theretofore unimaginable.

Prior to the Reformation, religious truth was preserved and disseminated through the hierarchy of the church and translated (literally, from the Latin language that was not commonly spoken) to the masses through the properly ordained clergy. The legal and sacramental structure of the church was viewed as the essential medium through which a person had access to Christ's grace and the possibility of salvation. Just as Jesus had mediated God to people, so too had the tradition held that the church took the place of Jesus in mediating God to the people. After the Reformation, however, people now had access to the Bible itself. The reformers and their adherents questioned the traditional authority of the church, including its clergy and sacramental practices (namely, baptism, Eucharist, confirmation, reconciliation, ordination, marriage, and anointing the sick), and argued that all they needed was the Bible. As reformers looked at the past theological tradition, including the weighty tomes of the scholastic theologians, they discovered that much of the tradition was actually extra-biblical. In other words, much theology introduced ideas that could not clearly be traced to or supported by the Bible. Since the same church authorities who were being rejected were seen as responsible for these extra-biblical ideas, much of the tradition as a whole came under the critical searchlight of reformed theologians.

On the question of salvation, where the past tradition had focused on such ideas as satisfaction, redemption, ransom, and substitutionary sacrifice, the reformers (and, particularly, Martin Luther) honed in on one major idea in Paul's letters: *justification*. Specifically, Luther struggled with Paul's Letter to the Romans, in which Paul speaks of the righteousness of God.[15] For Luther, this notion was repugnant until he interpreted that God's righteousness actually referred to God's merciful gift of faith whereby a sinner is made righteous.[16] Luther concluded that through faith only (that is, not through any human works or acts such as sacramental rites but through faith alone), the human being is justified by Jesus' saving work and is made righteous. Of this, Luther says:

> We should not look on Christ as an innocent private person (as the scholastics, Jerome, and others have done), a person who is holy and just in himself. It is true that Jesus Christ is a person who is very pure, but one cannot stop there. You have not yet understood even if you understand that he is God and man. But you will understand truly if you believe that the

> most pure and innocent person has been given to you by the Father to be pontiff and saviour, or rather to be your slave, who, stripping himself of his innocence and holiness, clothes himself with your sinful person, with your death and curse, becoming for you a victim and a curse, in order to deliver you from the curse of the law.[17]

And, while Luther's thinking about the mechanism of Jesus' salvific suffering was not structurally innovative, he expressed a tremendous pathos and gratitude for the act of Jesus' suffering itself. Paul Althaus' study of the salvation theology of Martin Luther captures this nuance well. Althaus says:

> Christ's sufferings are completely human. He suffers as an absolutely genuine man. Even though the depth of his personal agony on the cross cannot be measured, the fact that he suffers completely like any other man means it is still an analogy between the temptation which the godly experience in their conscience under God's wrath and the passion of Christ. He is a man who is tempted to the point of despair. He suffers God as his conscience bears the burden of the consciousness of guilt. For this reason, he is able to understand us men in the total depth of our need under God and help us in it ...

Christ has thus fully endured the horror of the anxiety of death, of being forsaken by God, of being under God's wrath. Luther gives a detailed description of the absolutely terrible hopelessness of the situation. Christ's suffering is, however, distinguished from our experience of wrath and of being forsaken by God by the fact that he does not suffer all this for himself but for us. He lovingly enters into the entire need of the sinner before God:

> He was moved both by his own desire and by the will of the father to be a friend of sinners. Thus he is forsaken by God and suffers God's wrath in our place. He takes our sins upon himself as though they were his own. In this way, he stands before God as a sinner among sinners and God treats him as such. Our salvation depends on Christ's thus taking our sins upon himself.[18]

While Luther established the basic emphasis on justification that would characterize Reformation attitudes toward salvation, John Calvin formalized it in his *Institutes of Christian Religion*. Calvin systematically explored the notion of human sin, degeneration, corruption of the free will, and the need for Christ to regenerate humanity (Book 2). Calvin then elaborated on the notions of regeneration, justification, election, and predestination (Book 3), in which he claimed that God justifies the elect according exclusively to God's own free will. Through the blameless sacrifice of Jesus, God "cloaks" sinful humanity in righteousness as if covering people with a cloth. Calvin argued that God imputes righteousness to the sinner and forgives sins, which begins a process of vivification (or regeneration) of the spirit. According to Calvin, the free will, once corrupted by sin, is now able to again do good (even though the good works do not actually merit salvation for us). The human being is justified through God's grace and is entirely dependent on God's election (or predetermined choice). In other words, God graces those whom God chooses to grace, and human beings have no say or influence in the matter. Calvin especially emphasized the need for Jesus' sacrifice in order to bring this about:

> The very nature of his death contains a striking truth. The cross was cursed, not only in the opinion of men, but by the carrying out of divine Law. So, Christ, while hanging on it, subjected himself to the curse. This had to be done so that the whole curse, which we deserved because of sin, might be taken from us by being transferred to him ... The apostle stated this even more plainly when he says that "God made him who had no sin to be sin for us, so that in him we might become the righteousness of God" (2 Cor. 5:21). The Son of God, though spotlessly pure, took upon himself the disgrace and shame of our iniquity, and in return clothed us with his purity. He seems to refer to the same thing when he says that God "condemned sin in sinful man" (Rom. 8:3) having destroyed the power of sin when it was transferred to him by imputation. The cross to which he was nailed was a symbol of this, as the apostle proclaims "Christ redeemed us from the curse of the law by becoming a curse for us, for it is written Cursed is everyone who is hung on a tree ... If Christ had not been a victim, we could have no certainty of his being our substitute, ransom, and propitiation. So blood is always mentioned whenever Scripture explains the way of salvation. The shedding of Christ's blood was not only for propitiation but for the cleansing of sin."[19]

As the Reformation progressed, variety, difference, and debate were the key features. Not only did the reformers not agree with the Roman Catholic Church, but they also did not always agree with one another. The conflicts were often political as well as ecclesial and theological in nature, leading to war and bloodshed. Eventually, a model of denominationalism was reached, in which Christians of different creeds lived according to their own precepts and accepted (even if begrudgingly) the beliefs of others. In this process, reformers, like the first Christians, were tasked with developing clear statements of their beliefs, called "confessions." In his research on salvation in reformation theology, David Wright summarizes the soteriology of several protestant confessional statements in the following way:[20]

1 Augsburg Confession (1530) – states that the *Son of God was truly born, suffered, was crucified, died and was buried in order to be a sacrifice not only for original sin but also for all other sins and to propitiate God's wrath.*
2 Genevan Confession (1536) – states that *it is Jesus Christ who is given to us by the Father, in order that in him we should recover all of which in ourselves we are deficient.*

3 Scots Confession (1560) – states that Christ's death, passion, and burial purchase for us *everlasting purgation and satisfaction.*
4 Belgic Confession (1560) – states that *our everlasting High Priest presented himself on our behalf before his Father in order to appease his wrath by his full satisfaction.*
5 Second Helvetic Confession (1566) – states that all that Christ did and endured for our sake by coming in the flesh reconciles the heavenly Father to all the faithful, expiates sins, disarms death, and shatters condemnation and hell.

In response to the reformers, the Roman Catholic Church convened its own council in order to respond to the theological and institutional challenges of the Protestant reformers. The Council of Trent (1545–47) spoke specifically to the questions of justification, the nature of humanity's righteousness, the nature of justifying faith, and the nature of salvation. As might be expected, the council strongly opposed Luther's notion of justification on the grounds of faith alone, in which righteousness is experienced by the human merely as a cloak covering sin. Trent argued that the human is justified in baptism and becomes regenerated in an interior way over time through participation in the sacramental life of the church. Hence, the Council of Trent reiterated the central role that the Roman Catholic Church continued to play in the administration of the sacraments, and thereby, in its administration of the merits of Christ's sacrifice.[21]

## Conclusion

Whether Catholic or Protestant, the Reformation era theologians generally adopted a much more personal approach to thinking about salvation. If the medieval thinkers were interested in explaining the mechanics of salvation from God's point of view, the Reformation era thinkers were interested in these same mechanics from humanity's point of view. As people challenged the traditional authority of the church and sought more autonomous approaches to their readings of the Bible, attention shifted to the issue of how people could understand God's saving merits personally, in their own lives. It took time for the reformers to adopt systematic treatments of their theological issues, and when they did, the questions of soteriology were diffused throughout their entire projects. The Roman Catholic Church, by contrast, continued to teach and articulate its specific understanding of grace as disseminated through the sacramental practices of the Church itself. While the Roman Catholic Church endeavored to correct the internal moral and institutional irregularities it had developed over the years, it nevertheless maintained its basic approach to understanding the role of the Church in dispensing the merit of Christ's death on the Cross.

Taking a step back from close consideration of these questions, today's reader may ask what these thinkers from hundreds of years ago mean for Christian believers in the present day. In answering this question, it is helpful to consider first that these complex ideas are today maintained in the official teachings of the various Christian denominations. Where one finds an emphasis on sacraments, as in the Roman Catholic Church for example, it is due to the Church's overarching belief that the sacraments are essential for the believer to access salvation through Jesus. Where conversely one finds an emphasis on the Bible or the teaching that one needs to be "born again," as in respectively mainstream Protestant and evangelical churches, it is due to the churches' basic belief that salvific truth is accessed only through the Bible or experienced only in the transformative experience of a dramatic faith conversion. These issues may seem esoteric and philosophical, but in fact they operate at a basic (even if unselfconscious) level in the hearts and minds of believers.

It is useful, furthermore, to recognize the great variability over the ages in how Christians have understood Jesus' death as saving human beings. This developmental tradition represents the efforts of living people in every era attempting to understand what it is they are claiming when they claim that Jesus is their Lord and Savior. The historical-political-geographical contexts contributed to the shape of this thought throughout the past ages. Moreover, today's context continues to pose new challenges for the question of salvation for Christians now. It is for this reason, therefore, that a historical-developmental consideration of soteriology requires both an awareness of the past traditions as well as an awareness of contemporary developments. It is to these more current soteriological questions that we now turn.

## Questions for review and discussion

1. Describe your understanding of soteriology in the biblical era. What concerns and issues helped drive and shape the way Christians of this era thought about Jesus' death?
2. How would you say these ideas were transformed in the patristic era? Were they significantly different in any way?
3. Compare trends in soteriology from the Middle Ages and the Reformation era. What would you say were the dominant characteristics of these eras?
4. Does this discussion help you understand any of the differences among Christian churches? Why were these differences enough to lead people to violence when they first occurred? What is at stake for Christians in how they understand and teach about Jesus?
5. Explain the dynamic relationship between believers and the shape of their beliefs.

## Resources

McIntyre, John. *The Shape of Soteriology: Studies in the Doctrine of the Death of Christ*. Edinburgh: T & T Clark, 1992.

Sheetes, S.J., John R., Ed. *The Theology of the Atonement: Readings in Soteriology*. Englewood Cliffs, New Jersey: Prentice Hall, 1967.

Sloyan, Gerard S. *Why Jesus Died*. Minneapolis: Fortress Press, 2004.

# 5 Soteriology, Part II

## Revisiting the Cross in the contemporary period

> Whoever grounds suffering in an almighty, alien One who ordains everything has to face the question of the justice of this God – and he must be shattered by it ... People who are shattered by this God as experienced as heteronomous, who allows evil as if he were possessed by our baser instincts, are people who think too much of God and too little of themselves.
>
> Dorothee Soelle[1]

### Introduction

The time period following the Reformation may be thought of as the "modern" period, beginning in the mid-eighteenth century. A summary of the main achievements and issues of the modern era is not helpful here because the past several centuries in Christian history have simply borne witness to too many relevant geographical contexts, changing technologies, advances in scientific knowledge, and so on, to consider meaningfully in brief form. A full consideration of this period, then, would best be undertaken by a broader discussion, such as that found in the treatment of the modern era in Alister McGrath's *Historical Theology*.[2] In the theological consideration of soteriology, however, a few key transitions in the modern period may still helpfully be identified: 1) changing models of authority; 2) the role of reason; 3) historical consciousness; and 4) a turn to experience.

The *changing models of authority* in the modern period stem largely from the power dynamic that shifted after the Protestant Reformation. The long outcome of this schismatic turn in the West was the diminishment of the ecclesial power of the Roman Catholic Church in Europe. The Protestant denominations, moreover, never achieved the sweeping breadth of unified religio-political power that the Roman church had at its apex. In addition, the shifting power of the church was accompanied by the shifting models of rule as Europe replaced (often quite bloodily) ancient monarchial regimes with revolutionary democratic governments. In the new American context, religious freedom, Christian denominationalism, and a growing sense of tolerance for religious pluralism carried the day. The effect of separating religious authority from political power was profound. Religious authorities had no means of enforcing "truth," and so religious truth became a matter subject to freer investigation.

Cultivated *reason* became in theory (and to some degree in practice) a tool available to any rational and learned person for the critical investigation of all areas of knowledge. The intellectual outcomes were speculative inquiry, broader popular learning, and ultimately greater individual freedom in the assessment of religious truth claims. People were suddenly liberated from believing what the "authorities" told them. Now, they could read the Bible for themselves, think about it constructively, and make rational judgments about what they discovered. This cultural movement that prized the use of reason is referred to as the "Enlightenment." Since the Enlightenment gave priority to truths that could be demonstrated or proven through reason *alone* (that is, apart from special revelation), the impact on Christian beliefs was dramatic.

Among the aspects of Christianity that the Enlightenment thinkers critiqued were claims about the miracles Jesus performed; the notion of revelation itself; the idea that the Bible contained special truth not elsewhere available; and the idea of Jesus' Resurrection. Since none of these claims could be demonstrated through logical proofs or empirical studies, many Enlightenment thinkers began to revise their understanding of the identity and meaning of Jesus. Perhaps best exemplified in Immanuel Kant's (1724–1804) work *Religion Within the Limits of Reason Alone*, Enlightenment thinkers turned to a model of Jesus as moral exemplar and teacher par excellence. They downplayed the miraculous aspects of the traditional claims about his death and Resurrection (since it could not be proven and in fact defied reason), and replaced it with a model of Jesus as a figure who is redemptive in virtue of the excellence of his humanity alone. In making this shift, people began to differentiate between Jesus as known through faith (i.e., the traditional claims about Jesus as savior and so on), and the "historical" Jesus as known through biblical, contextual, and archeological research.[3] Efforts at distinguishing, integrating, and researching Christology in this fashion continue to this day.[4]

The new *historical consciousness* that was brought to the study of Christian religion affected not only the way in which theologians studied the Bible and the life of Jesus, but also introduced a critical historical study of the development of the church and the doctrines the churches teach and maintain. Far from revealing a static or unchanging institution and its beliefs, historical-critical awareness of religion has shown that faith traditions are dynamic and always reflective of era and context. Understanding *tradition*, therefore, requires the complementary component of understanding the geo-political-historical situation in which the tradition is (or was) lived by a community of believers.

Since at least the nineteenth century, this awareness has resulted in a profound *turn to concrete human experience* in Christian theological studies. While it was always implicitly important, in the contemporary era there has been a self-conscious awareness of the context of daily life in which people indelibly experience religious faith. Sometimes faith deeply connects with experience, which in turn reinforces belief; other times faith contrasts with lived experience, resulting in a critical dialectic between religious belief and the rest of one's life. This happens at the personal as well as at the corporate level. An example, here, might be the disconnect that comes from: 1) Christian claims about the creation of life as derived from literal readings of the Bible's Book of Genesis; and 2) a modern scientific understanding of natural history. Another example might be: 1) Christian claims about the Kingdom of God as initiated in the life of Jesus; and 2) the radical evil of modern warfare and the potential for global, nuclear annihilation. In the case of contrast, a more "suspicious" attitude has characterized some of the major theological voices of the past several decades. In all cases, theologians have been tasked to think more concretely about the nature of Christian truth claims vis-à-vis the real-life experiences of the community of believers.

## Soteriology in the modern period

As a result of these turns, contemporary theology represents a broad spectrum of "types" and commitments. Moreover, how Jesus is understood and communicated as *savior*, then, depends largely on the Christian denomination, social location, and the hermeneutical (or interpretive) priorities of the theologian or the community doing the theology. It should be said at the outset that many Christian believers might not employ the technical theological language used in this book to describe their beliefs. Nevertheless, as contemporary persons, their faith has been influenced (even if unaware) by several trends:[5] 1) their beliefs are likely to have been shaped by some critical-historical awareness; 2) they live in a religiously plural context, so they must understand their beliefs, at the very least, as existing in the midst of competing religious worldviews; 3) contemporary Christian belief is, furthermore, disinclined to approach God in the highly philosophical tones of the scholastics; it is by contrast much more "personalist" and connected to an individual sense of interior spirituality; 4) contemporary Christian belief has been enhanced by more widespread, scholarly understanding of the Bible; and 5) while it seeks better and more reliable foundations, contemporary belief is also marked by a suspicion of authority and tradition (especially in the dual light of a more religiously educated body of faithful and the many public failures and scandals of the institutional churches).

The meaning of the central Christian claim that Jesus died on the Cross for humanity's sins is therefore highly dependent on the primary outlook of the theologian or community interpreting that doctrine. Orthodox and neo-orthodox theologians, especially when they speak from positions of authority in the institutional context of church leadership, will continue to affirm soteriology in one or more of the classic formulae considered in the previous chapter: sacrifice, ransom, substitution, satisfaction, moral guidance. Oppositional theologies that openly reject the institutional church will often deny the claim that the sacrifice on the Cross is ontologically (or fundamentally) salvific, although they may (with the Enlightenment thinkers) continue to affirm that it has "saving" merit as a moral example.

It is in the middle ground, in the arena of what is called "revisionist" theology, where one finds today an abundance of creative thought about the saving effect of the Cross and the work of Jesus. It is also this arena of theology that is most attentive to a critical analysis of culture and its relevance to the claims of the faith tradition. These approaches to theology take seriously revelation in the Bible, although the interpretive principles that guide the use of scripture may result in a wide spectrum of interpretations and uses of the Bible. Middle-ground approaches tend to be tolerant of religious plurality, even within the Christian faith tradition. They are suspicious of classical formulae, in the sense that they will seek out hidden biases, and they are earnest about attaching truth claims to the intimate realities of human experience at individual and social levels. Contemporary revisionist theologies that are expressly concerned with soteriology, moreover, will attend to at least three prominent categories (among possible others) that have indelibly marked today's experientially based Christian dialogue about salvation. These include: 1) militarism, war, and violence in the twentieth and twenty-first centuries; 2) systemic social oppression, including the historical oppression of women; and 3) bodies, nature, and the welfare of the earth itself. Here a closer consideration of each is in order.

## Violence and war

In his work *A Century of War: The History of Worldwide Conflict in the 20th Century*,[6] David Miller evaluates eight major international conflicts, twenty-five regional conflicts and major civil wars, and eleven insurgencies and insurrections. Accompanied by photographic detail, Miller explores the history of twentieth-century conflicts, the cost to national treasuries, and the incomprehensible death toll (as far as it is known) of these wars and battles. Despite the scope of the book, Miller chillingly observes that conflict in the past century was so far flung and pervasive that his own work can only survey *some* of the conflicts people endured. He claims, "it is doubtful if there has been one day in the century when there has not been at least one conflict somewhere in the world, and frequently more."[7]

The extent of war in the past century and into the first decades of the present one is vast. The First (1914–18) and Second (1939–45) World Wars occurred on an unprecedented, global scale. The combined, estimated military dead of the First World War is over nine million people, with nineteen million more wounded.[8] In the Second World War, over thirteen million (combined Axis and Allied) military died, and over twenty-five million more were wounded.[9] An estimated six million Jews were murdered in the Holocaust, alongside five million more non-Jewish citizens. Hundreds of thousands died and were wounded when the United States dropped atom bombs on Hiroshima and Nagasaki, Japan. Moreover, in the dozens of regional and civil wars that raged, millions more lives have been lost, destroyed, and grieved.

The staggering numbers of military lives lost in the past century to warfare is gravely compounded by the astounding reality of genocides by the murderous dictators behind these conflicts. The extent of the suffering and loss of civilian lives is almost impossible to grasp meaningfully. For example, in Piero Scaruffi's survey of twentieth-century genocides, he credits Mao Ze-Dong with somewhere between fifty and seventy-eight million Chinese dead.[10] In another example, Terry Stafford's research into the Soviet Gulag suggests that over sixty-one million people were killed under Joseph Stalin's extermination policies. Stafford drives home the point in his description of the transportation process to the Gulag during this reign of terror. Prisoners on ships were often frozen in the ice, later to be fed to the living or tossed aside to decompose eventually in the summer thaw. He goes on:[11]

> Other accounts tell us that while the secret police administered the operation of the camps, inside the barracks criminal leaders ruled, abusing the weak. Women in the Gulag were almost always considered prey. They were often raped on transport ships or in railroad cars, even before they reached the camps. Upon arrival at their destination they would be paraded naked in front of camp officials, who would select their favorites to provide sexual favors to their new masters. Women not selected became "prizes" for male (and sometimes female) inmates. The pitiful creatures inhabiting the world of the Gulag suffered from starvation, exhaustion, exposure, and physical abuse on a routine basis. Uncooperative prisoners, of either sex, might be subjected to isolation, impalement, genital mutilation, or perhaps more mercifully, a bullet to the brain.

In the context of the millions tortured, abused, raped, and killed at the hands of these and others (Leopold II of Belgium, Hideki Tojo of Japan, Pol Pot of Camobodia, Saddam Hussein of Iraq, and so on), suffering in the twentieth and twenty-first centuries takes on a vast corporate quality, even while the horrors of that suffering must be considered at the level of individual human experience in order to begin to approach its significance.

What is more, modern warfare technology has made killing easier and swifter and at a greater scale than ever before in history. As Catherine Keller so astutely recognizes in her work *Apocalypse Now and Then*,[12] human beings now have the power to destroy life itself. For the many who remember the Cuban Missile Crisis and the Cold War, the threat of annihilation was palpable and real. Today, that threat continues with the ongoing development and acquisition of nuclear armaments, especially in the Middle East, which put at risk literally everyone on the planet. With the present threat of terrorism by dozens of known and operational organizations worldwide (who actively organize around such stated goals as the destruction of economies, nations, and governments), people today experience a legacy of violence and war that often leads to a sense of apocalyptic despair.

In light of this violence, Christian theologians of the past century have been challenged to relate their doctrine of salvation in Christ to the historical reality of suffering in their midst. Three exemplary figures in this integrative task include Dietrich Bonhoeffer (1906–45), Jürgen Moltmann (b. 1926), and Dorothee Soelle (1929–2003). All three German theologians were tasked to consider Christian faith in the light of the atrocities of the Second World War and the Holocaust in their native land. Bonhoeffer himself was imprisoned and executed by the Nazis in 1945. His *Letters and Papers from Prison* bear witness to the challenge of making sense of Christian faith and ethics in light of the modern person's ambivalent experience. His own life was marked by the complexity of a basic endorsement of pacifism that, under the extreme circumstances of the Holocaust, gave way to Bonhoeffer's own participation in a plot to assassinate Hitler. For this, he himself was martyred.

Jürgen Moltmann, conscripted into the German army in 1944, surrendered to British troops and endured life as a prisoner of war between 1945 and 1948. His experiences led him to craft a theology that would address the specific needs and concerns of those of his generation who survived the war. Moltmann developed a "theology of hope," in which he focused on salvation in *eschatological* terms. "Eschatological" refers to the study of the "end times" or "last things" in Christian theology. Eschatology focuses on discussions of heaven and afterlife, and Moltmann's work helped to reframe historical evil in the context of the unlimited possibilities of the future that remain God's sole domain. Other German theologians, influenced by Hegelian dialectical philosophy, such as Reinhold Neibuhr and Wolfhart Pannenberg, similarly took up the question of history, evil, and the possibility of redemption. Each in his own right was driven to try to understand how God could bring about salvation in a world so rife with inescapable wickedness and suffering.

Dorothee Soelle's consideration of the subject reached beyond the traditional boundaries of Christian language to try to understand God in the face of suffering. For most of the tradition, God was (and is) described as unchanging and immutable, thereby rendering God also impassable (or unable to suffer). These attributes were seen as flowing naturally from the claim that God is all-powerful and absolute. But, for Soelle, it is unacceptable to fashion God in glorious, heavenly splendor while people suffer, such as they suffered in Auschwitz. The lived experience of the Holocaust caused Soelle to reevaluate the whole Christian schema that maintained God as simultaneously demanding human suffering (as penalty for sin) and also providing the one who would suffer (that is, Jesus). This, for Soelle, is "theological sadism," and her critique of it is stark:

> Who wants such a God? Who gains anything from him? What kind of people must those be whose highest being sees his honor in practicing retaliation in a ratio of one to 100? Why, in such a theology, should Jesus "suffer at God's hands"? Did the victims at Auschwitz die at God's hands, and not because of Cyclone Beta, which the IG-Farben Company manufactured for a few cents a dose? Was he on the side of the executioner – or still on the side of the dying? When you look at human suffering concretely you destroy all innocence, all neutrality, every attempt to say, "It wasn't I; there was nothing I could do; I didn't know." In the face of suffering you

> are either with the victim or the executioner – there is no other option. Therefore the explanation of suffering that looks away from the victim and identifies itself with a righteousness that is supposed to stand behind the suffering has already taken a step in the direction of theological sadism, which wants to understand God as the torturer.[13]

Because Soelle could not accept God as torturer, she was driven to conclude that if God is anything at all, God must actually be with the powerless victims of senseless suffering. In the Crucifixion, God is with Jesus. As she says, "God is not in heaven; he is hanging on the cross."[14] There is no God, then, who can or could have swept in and stopped Auschwitz, but there are human beings who can be with those who suffer so that suffering itself is not *de facto* all that is. Because God is with people in their suffering, suffering can also be endured in hope:

> In this sense those who suffer in vain and without respect depend on those who suffer in accord with justice. If there were no one who said, "I die, but I shall live," no one who said, "I and the Father are one," then there would be no hope for those who suffer mute and devoid of hoping. All suffering would then be senseless, destructive pain that could not be worked on, all grief would be "worldly grief" and would lead to death. But we know of people who have lived differently, suffered differently. There is a history of resurrections, which has vicarious significance. A person's resurrection is no personal privilege for himself alone – even if he is called Jesus of Nazareth. It contains within itself hope for all, for everything.[15]

Dorothee Soelle, grounded in the reality of profound yet senseless human suffering, suggests a considerable redefinition of the Christian doctrine of resurrection. Resurrection for Soelle is framed as hope, in spite of suffering, made possible because the sufferer has somehow experienced God as also present in his or her pain. There is no Deity to come in and correct sin and evil in Soelle's theology; that task is the humans', who either act out of hope in solidarity with those who suffer or despairingly do not act and thus become complicit in others' suffering.

Such a redefinition is a constructive example of how lived experience contributes to the contemporary Christian thought on Jesus' saving work. The believing community, situated in the hardcore facts of social and historical contexts, cannot avoid or gloss over suffering. Christian thinking on Jesus' life and death, then, is bound to take seriously the reality of suffering and to reconcile it (if possible) with the story of Jesus' own suffering and dying.

## Oppression

The effort at reconciling Jesus' life and death is found in another experientially based dimension of modern Christian thinking, namely, liberation theologies. In his work "Theology in a Suffering World,"[16] Jon Sobrino argues that all theology is ineluctably contextually based. Every effort at thinking as a Christian or living Christian faith happens somewhere specific, sometime specific, and has particular local colorations as well as superstructural conditions (geographic locations and political systems, for example). Yet, underlying the specific, local, and superstructural aspects of context is the more fundamental, pervasive, and immediate reality of suffering. People *en masse* suffer, and so the first context that any experientially based theology must consider is suffering itself.

Throughout history Christian theology has maintained a relationship with the suffering world at various levels. First, Christians recognize natural suffering as a reality (such as that brought about by disease, drought, famine, earthquakes, and so on). At another level, Christian theology has reflected on the harmfulness of suffering and its causes (such as sin and human wickedness). At the level of biblical revelation and the Jesus experience, Christians have contemplated how suffering is at once undesirable by God yet potentially constructive as a moral corrective. Finally, Christians (such as Moltmann, described above) have considered the eschatological end of suffering that will occur in the fullness of God's time. Sobrino argues that in the reflection on suffering, Christians are required to address both: 1) the fundamental forms of human suffering (individual, political, corporate, historical, metaphysical); and also 2) the origin of suffering and how we can co-exist with it until it is ended.

In today's world, Sobrino contends that the kind of suffering that has to be addressed is the historical suffering of the world's poor. In order to understand this level of suffering, Christians must come to a critical recognition of systemic poverty as the outcome of global dynamics of power between the first and developing worlds and between the rich and the poorer classes. Sobrino further contends that historical suffering of the poor is precisely the kind of suffering that God in the Bible rejects and opposes. Thus, for a contemporary Christian theology to be relevant in a suffering world, its theology must address head on the suffering of humanity as it is (and why it is). To fail to do so is to render the entire theological enterprise questionable.

Sobrino is here discussing the broad commitment of liberation theologies to address the concrete social-political conditions that lead to suffering. This commitment is based on readings of the Bible (such as are found in Exodus, the prophets, and Jesus' ministry to the poor in the Gospels), in which God is portrayed as an actor in the cause of human liberation. From such biblical readings, liberation theologians (taking their cue from Gustavo Guttierrez, known as the father of "liberation theology") conclude that God makes a "preferential option for the poor." Thus, from the liberationist perspective, wherever the poor may be found in any given context, that is where God's sympathies lie. Put another way, these thinkers see in the Bible evidence that God does not want poverty and openly militates against the structures that cause it.

Liberation perspectives, then, may be found emerging from a whole range of population subsets for which a case can be made that systemic, historical oppressions have occurred. Some of the first and clearest voices among liberation theologians came from Central and South America in the mid-twentieth centuries when bishops, pastors, and missionaries attempted to meet the needs of the terribly impoverished and vulnerable masses. Today, liberation theologies have expanded all over the developing world as well as among minority groups of the first world.

As liberation theologians strive for the liberation from unjust social structures that cause systemic poverty and suffering, salvation is frequently described in "this-worldly" terms. The eschatological goals of heaven and resurrection are not denied, but they are relegated to the realm of things that people cannot control. Liberation theologies are thus "praxis" driven, which means they focus on the connections between experience, theoretical understanding of the causes of suffering, and corrective action to improve upon the conditions of daily life. Salvation, they will argue, begins with the goal of saving peoples' actual lives in tangible ways: the procurement of food, water, and medicine; the possibility of sustainable employment; and the right to the life and dignity of one's body.

A key insight among all liberation theologies is that the Christian faith tradition is not only required to respond to suffering but that it has also (both intentionally and at times unwittingly) been employed historically to create or endorse conditions of suffering. For example, in the biblical letter of First Timothy, chapter six issues rules for the conduct of slaves. Rather than encourage slaves to seek their freedom, this biblical text encourages slaves to be obedient and respectful of their masters so that the Christian teaching may not earn a bad name for itself. Texts such as this and Paul's letter to Philemon were once used to justify slavery, despite the fact that the Bible also descries slavery in the story of the exodus. When the Bible or some aspect of the faith tradition is used as a tool of oppression, it is particularly dangerous because the oppression in that instance is touted as divinely willed or sanctioned. For, if something is alleged and believed to come from God, then it is not only right to do that thing but also encouraged.

Dangerous uses of the tradition are perhaps most keenly felt and broadly recognized in the area of feminist liberation theologies. These theologies have critically evaluated the biblical, theological, and ecclesial traditions in an effort to understand and redress women's marginalization, exclusion, or oppression within Christian religion and Western society. On the one hand, insofar as feminists may be Christians, their theologies are religiously motivated to correct grievous error in the faith tradition of which they are a part. On the other hand, insofar as feminist theologians recognize the interplay between Christianity and the entire reality of Western culture, they are socially and politically motivated to expose how religious oppression contributes to other types of social exclusions and oppression (such as the long legacy in the West – until the twentieth century – of denying women the right to vote on the basis of religious and philosophical claims about the inadequacy of women's minds and souls).

As feminist theologians have explored the causes of women's deep and multifaceted social oppressions, they have discovered a reality that is cross-cultural and trans-historical. The reality is characterized by many features, including, but not limited to: 1) exclusion from public dialogue and relegation to the domestic sphere; 2) restriction from education; 3) limitation or lack of opportunities for employment; 4) limitation or lack of opportunities for participation, study, and voice in the formal structures of church leadership; 5) relegation to legal status as the property of husbands or male relatives; and 6) vulnerability to sexual and domestic violence with no avenues for recourse. It would be an error to suggest that the Christian faith was singularly responsible for women's suffering in these ways. Yet, feminists have demonstrated well[17] that Christianity contributed to these social conditions in the West through a basically negative attitude toward women, derived in the first instance from key source material, such as this biblical passage from First Timothy 2:11–15:

> A woman must receive instruction silently and under complete control. I do not permit a woman to teach or have authority over a man. She must be quiet. For Adam was formed first, then Eve. Further, Adam was not deceived, but the woman was deceived and transgressed. But, she will be saved through motherhood, provided women persevere in faith and love and holiness, with self-control.

As feminists have attempted to understand and end women's suffering, they have been challenged to evaluate Christian doctrine in light of women's lived experience. Jesus' own suffering has been a key concern, and the question that has been raised is: *can a male savior save women*? Among the more creative responders to this question is the womanist[18] theologian Delores Williams, in her work *Sisters in the Wilderness.*[19] In this work, Williams explores this question from the perspective of African-American women's history and the legacy of the slave experience of the black community.

Williams recovers the biblical figure of Hagar (Genesis 16, 21) and draws parallels between: 1) the Egyptian handmaid's experience as a sexual surrogate for Abraham and Sarah;[20] and 2) the experiences of enslaved black women in America. Williams argues that in both cases, the women were forced to endure surrogate roles for the advantage of their oppressors. In the case of American slaves, the surrogacy involved domestic labor (care for white homes, families, and children); field labor; and sexual surrogacy (both for the reproduction of more slaves and also the pleasure of slaveholders). In light of this history, Williams asks whether Jesus' death, classically framed as a surrogate sacrifice, can be salvific for black women in the United States' historical context. (At stake, of course, is the inference that if Jesus' suffering was a good and holy thing then so also might the suffering of black women be a good and holy thing.) Williams responds to this question with a definitive "no!" For Williams, it is not Jesus' death and surrogate suffering that are salvific but rather his life. Williams argues that Jesus' life exemplified ministries of healing, compassion, and resistance to oppression; it is this life (and not Jesus' sorrowful and unjust death) that black women can turn to in the ongoing struggle for survival. Jesus' death and surrogate suffering, for Williams, together represent a profound act of cruelty and violence that in no way represents God's will for Jesus. Jesus' Resurrection is God's way of recovering and ensuring the message of Jesus' life, but this is in spite of his death and not because of it.

Drawing similar conclusions about the value of violence and suffering, liberation theologies have arisen across a broad spectrum. African, Asian, Latin American, Hispanic, feminist, black, womanist, mujerisa,[21] and queer theologies are all endeavors to speak out against poverty and oppression in all its expressions. The broad goal is twofold: 1) to create a more just society by exposing aspects of Christian religion that have contributed to suffering; and 2) to reclaim sources within Christian religion that empower people to resist and overcome suffering. The praxis of liberation theologies is played out in real time and is directed toward concrete social action. These theologies reject sacrificial death, primarily because they are too intimate with the ongoing reality of sacrificial death among the communities for whom they speak. In liberationist work, then, the saving power of Jesus' life and death must be constructively revisited and reinterpreted in light of the lived struggle of oppressed people striving for security and meaningful lives.

## Environment

When suffering is considered in concrete, experiential terms, the focus inevitably turns to the body. For, it is in the body that suffering is principally endured. When the focus is the body, though, a whole throng of new issues surface. Such issues include, for example, agriculture and the production of food. How is food grown? Who grows it? What sorts of pesticides are used in its production, and what are the effects of these chemicals on the surrounding flora, fauna, soil, and water quality? What are the communities like around food production? How is the food packaged and preserved? How is it transported and distributed? What resources are expended in the transportation of food across great distances? How much food is lost in the transportation itself? Do those who grow food have an opportunity to eat it? Who enjoys food? Who profits from it? And on and on.

Questions such as these, which may not at first blush seem religious in nature, take on a rich theological significance when one is asking about the welfare of bodies. These questions begin often with a concern for *human* bodies, but they naturally expand to a consideration of other types of bodies: animal bodies, plant bodies, insect bodies, bodies of water, bodies of land and soil. As even grade schoolchildren can report, bodies of all kinds within an ecosystem are fundamentally interconnected and interdependent upon one another for their survival. When oppression is analyzed at its most basic levels, one finds that it is access and control over the fundamental resource of bodies that is at stake.

Many theologians, liberationist and otherwise, have thus turned their attention to explicitly ecological concerns. They recognize that environmental abuse stemming from war, militarism, violence, over-consumption, industrial agriculture, land encroachment, and so on, have contributed to an unsustainable way of life for human beings and other creatures. They further argue that the Christian theological tradition must oppose such unsustainable patterns out of the belief that the world is God's good creation. Although proper understanding of the manner in which God creates is debated among Christians, most agree that the world comes into its being and is sustained by a free and ongoing act of creation. Moreover, many recognize that the bodies of creation are de facto imbued with a sacred quality because God has intentionally brought them about. To abuse bodies is therefore an indirect abuse of God.

What is more, for some, the natural world should be understood not only as God's creation but also as an aspect of the very God. Sallie McFague, for example, employs the pan*en*theistic (meaning that God is *in* everything, as opposed to pantheistic meaning that God *is* everything) metaphor of the world as God's body. In her landmark work *The Body of God*, McFague uses this language to establish a theological response to modern ecological crisis.

McFague focuses her argument on the physical space that all embodied creatures require. If salvation in the body of God is to be experienced, it will have to be in the physical space of our planet. Focusing on space is a corrective lens for McFague because it is the ultimate democratizing principle. Space puts human beings on par with other creatures on the planet. Everything that exists needs space to survive. Moreover, justice issues can be seen most through the lens of physical space; if we do not have physical space to be, we do not have anything. Everything needs enough good space to survive, and those who take more than their share are shown to be blatantly in the wrong. The focus on space, then, reminds people that the earth is our home, it is our place. It is, thus, on earth (and not some heavenly alternative) where salvation must occur. It is on the earth, moreover, where Jesus reveals to Christians, within the total cosmic body of God, what liberating love might be.

For McFague, theology drawn from an organic model of God has several salvific characteristics. Such a theology reminds us that: 1) humans are "latecomers" to the planet and not the centerpiece of the cosmic story; 2) Creation is not a past-tense event but an ongoing act of God; 3) from an ecological perspective, everything is interrelated; 4) life in the universe exists on a continuum (which means that although human life may be more complex than that of other animals, it is not substantially different); and finally 5) Creation is common and public – we all share the same origin and the same destiny.[22]

McFague's work exemplifies the contemporary theological turn to bodies and their environments. In this turn, soteriology has become detached from the classical discussions of salvation that focus on heaven and redemption. By refocusing the question of salvation in bodily terms, sin becomes described as usurpation and abuse of space and resources. Jesus' crucifixion becomes not the saving sacrifice but rather an analog and critique of the "crucifixion" of other bodies. Resurrection is redefined in terms of hope and resistance to other such violence. And, finally, salvation in turn is viewed as corrected, spatially balanced, and ecologically responsible living.

## Conclusion

As this and the previous chapter have shown, soteriology throughout the ages has reflected broad cultural and philosophical influences and situations. These, of course, have been in flux from one era to the next. The result is that Christian understanding of sin, suffering, and salvation has never enjoyed one exclusive, exhaustive, or definitive theological explanation – not in the Bible, not in the patristic age, not during the scholastic period, not during the Reformation, not during the Enlightenment, and not during the contemporary era. The need for salvation is largely understood vis-à-vis human suffering, and the experience of suffering is largely dependent upon contingent factors in the changing social context.

For Christians who are not theological specialists, the history of thinking about the saving meaning of Jesus might seem at first foreign or abstract. It might be fair to ask about the relevance of what people thought hundreds of years ago. By way of response, thinking about the long tradition of trying to understand Jesus' life and death reveals several important features of Christian life and practice. First, it reveals that part of the Christian faith experience is attempting to understand Jesus and the ongoing impact his story has on one's life as a believer. That experience can only be felt in the present moment and in one's own skin, so to speak. But, the experience of trying to understand Jesus' meaning is what connects Christians across time. By looking at the long tradition, Christian people are invited into a dynamic dialogue with their foremothers and forefathers in faith. Second, revisiting the tradition reveals that theological doctrine has mostly been forged around the various efforts of the church, at any point in time, to make sense of people's suffering at both the individual and social levels. To ask about Jesus as savior was and is to ask about sin and its causes; to consider the end of sin; to understand pain, death, bereavement; and ultimately to express hope that there is something more than this. For people in the immediacy of their own struggles, participation in this theological dialogue is helpful in two fundamental ways: 1) one comes to appreciate the developmental rather than the fixed nature of faith; and 2) one becomes a conversation partner about the meaning of his or her own suffering, and the suffering of the world, in one's own terms and context. The inadequacy of past formulae to explain suffering demonstrates time and again that religious faith holds no easy or absolute answers for all ages. What lasts throughout the ages is the human search for meaning and hope in light of suffering. Religion represents a historical composite of wisdom and experience from which to draw, even while people are challenged evermore to generate intelligible answers for themselves.

## Questions for discussion and review

1 Describe the changing nature of religious authority in the modern era.
2 Describe your modern context. What elements of it might sharply alter classical approaches to religious dialogue?
3 How do you think war, oppression, and ecological crisis do or should reframe the ways we think about suffering?
4 Are these realities different today than in previous eras? If so, how?
5 How might you constructively employ the history of salvation theologies in conversation with someone who was questioning the meaning of her own suffering today?

## Resources

Briggs, Sheila, et al., Eds. *Oxford Handbook of Feminist Theology*. New York and Oxford: Oxford University Press, 2012.
Coker, Christopher. *War and the 20th Century: A Study of War and Modern Consciousness*. London and Washington: Brassey's, 1994.
Cooper, David E. and Joy A. Palmer, Eds. *Spirit of the Environment: Religion, Value, and Environmental Concern*. London and New York: Routledge, 1998.
Herzog, Frederick, Ed. *The Future of Hope: Theology as Eschatology*. New York: Herder & Herder, 1970.
Ruether, Rosemary Radford. *Christianity and Social Systems: Historical Constructions and Ethical Challenges*. Lanham, Maryland: Rowman & Littlefield, 2009.
Soelle, Dorothee. *Dorothee Soelle: Essential Writings*. Maryknoll, New York: Orbis Books, 2006.

# 6 Death in comparative perspective

> In order to be at peace, it is necessary to find a sense of history – that you are both part of what has come before and part of what is yet to come. Being thus surrounded, you are not alone; and the sense of urgency that pervades the present is put in perspective. Do not frivolously use the time that is yours to spend. Cherish it, that each day may bring new growth, insight, and awareness. Use this growth not selfishly, but rather in service of what may be, in the future tide of time. Never allow a day to pass that did not add to what was understood before. Let each day be a stone in the path of growth. Do not rest until what was intended has been done. But remember – go as slowly as is necessary in order to sustain a steady pace; do not expend energy in waste. Finally, do not allow the illusory urgencies of the immediate to distract you from your vision of the eternal ...
>
> Elisabeth Kubler-Ross[1]

## Introduction

Suffering, grieving, and dying are universal human experiences. Tombs and funerary objects found across the globe bear witness to the tenderness of the human attitude toward death. In the ancient Near Eastern lands of Mesopotamia, the Levant, and Egypt, rich traditions for thinking about the meaning of human life and death preexisted even the ancient Hebraic attitudes recorded in the Bible. In Greek and Roman cultures, which constituted the political and social context of Christianity's earliest centuries, equally rich considerations of life and death permeated their philosophical, poetic, and religious discourses. The biblical attitudes towards death (discussed in Chapters 2 and 3) as well as the post-biblical theological developments in Christian thinking (discussed in Chapters 4 and 5) occurred in dialogue with, and sometimes in response to, broader social constructions of the meaning of death. Such constructions informed not only how death was understood but also the practices for burial and customs for mourning.

From a theological perspective, it is helpful to consider attitudes outside one's own tradition in relationship to general aspects of one's culture as well as other religious traditions. Such comparative considerations help to establish a broad and long view of one's faith as a constituent and dialogical part of history and culture itself. A single religious tradition may offer a comprehensive worldview that internally makes sense from within the religion itself. Yet, insofar as multiple religions and secular perspectives co-exist, no single tradition is capable of speaking to all human thought and experience of death. It is thus illuminating to consider what others are saying about death. In addition, viewing one's own tradition from a non-believer's perspective may lead to new insight about one's own faith.

It is further fascinating to consider that all religious and secular traditions make their claims about life and death from the living side of the equation. Even Christianity, which speaks of direct experience of Jesus' Resurrection, must interpret and theologize about that resurrection by people who are alive. As such, all religious claims about the ultimate meaning of life, the death experience, and what comes after life must be thought of as (to some degree) speculative and interpretive in nature (rather than absolute). Again, a broad consideration of multiple traditions can reveal commonalities as well as differences that pervade the anticipatory experience of death and the great beyond.

From a caregiving perspective, it is helpful to consider multiple religious traditions because the people one encounters professionally come from all walks of life and all religious faiths. Since religious traditions help to shape and inform the way people experience sickness, death, and bereavement, it is imperative for the caregiver to be conscientious about the interpretive frameworks and beliefs of their clients. Of course, it is an unlikely and unrealistic expectation that caregivers will all be comparative religion experts as well as skilled nurses, doctors, social workers, and so on. But, it is possible for people in the helping professions to be sensitive to the diversity that abounds in religious beliefs as well as attentive to the fact that beliefs have dramatic impact on the way people understand their suffering, prepare for death, and experience the loss of others.

There are many fine scholarly and clinical treatments of suffering and dying in cross-cultural perspective, some of which will be identified at the end of this chapter. Interested readers should pursue additional reading to explore death in ancient Near Eastern thought; indigenous religions of Africa, Australia, and North and South America; modern secular thought; futurist thought (such as the "transhumanist" movement); and others. This chapter will be limited to a comparative consideration of only five major religious perspectives: Judaism, Islam, Hinduism, Buddhism, and Taoism.

## Abrahamic faiths: Judaism and Islam

The faiths of Judaism, Christianity, and Islam are related as cousin faiths. Beginning with Judaism, each of these religions claims its origins in God's call of Abraham. From Abraham's lineage came these three great monotheistic religions. They share in common a belief in the oneness of God, although they differ in how they understand God's singleness as well as how God revealed himself to human beings in history. In the previous chapters, we have considered at length a Christian understanding of God's revelation in Jesus and how this revelation explains human suffering and dying. In this chapter, we will look in brief form at the basic teachings of Judaism and Islam pertaining to humanity's ultimate experiences of limit and loss.

## *Judaism*

Judaism is both a religion and a culture. Its origins date back to the third millennium BCE, and its early history and beliefs are recounted in the Hebrew Bible (as discussed in Chapter 2). Modern-day Judaism thus traces its heritage back thousands of years. There are about fifteen million Jews worldwide, although Judaism continues to have a special association with the biblical land of Israel, which is today the state of Israel. Some Jews are religiously observant, while others recognize their Judaism only as an ethnic and cultural heritage. Judaism is today represented by three major classifications: Orthodox, Conservative, or Reformed. There are also many secular Jewish institutions and organizations that promote study and understanding of the riches of Jewish culture as well as the welfare of Jewish people in the light of Judaism's history of profound religious persecution, especially in the twentieth-century experience of the Shoah.

Theologically, Judaism is rooted in the Hebrew Bible (called the Tanakh). Study of the Hebrew Bible is complemented by study of the Talmud, an important rabbinical text that discusses and interprets Jewish law. Jewish worship occurs in the context of the synagogue. Judaism is the first of the three Abrahamic religions (followed by Christianity and Islam), and is the first to articulate belief in one God.

For Judaism, the one God is understood as creating a covenantal relationship with the Jewish people, expressed foremost in the law which the people follow and by which they are bound to God. Since the law is believed to be God-given (as opposed to derived from human wisdom alone), Judaism has understood Jewish people as "chosen" to exist in this special covenant relationship. The Hebrew Bible (for example, in Hosea and the Song of Songs) sometimes likens this covenantal relationship between God and Israel to a marital relationship between a husband and wife.

The biblical Hebrew faith places its emphasis on life rather than death. This emphasis is derived from the belief in the essential goodness of God's creation. The good life is characterized by health, longevity, fecundity, and the ability to praise, worship, and serve God. The older texts of the Hebrew Bible discuss death in matter-of-fact terms and do not develop an elaborate theological apparatus for considering heaven or afterlife. In fact, discussion of afterlife or resurrection is a phenomenon that emerges in the post-exilic literature (such as in the Book of Ezekiel and the Book of Job), during a period of oppression and frustration with the seeming lack of justice in the present world.

As such, the Jewish traditions over the ages concerning death and suffering have not been absolute. This is manifested today in the different attitudes toward death and afterlife found among Orthodox, Conservative, and Reformed Jews. Reformed Judaism tends not to emphasize belief in a resurrection of the body, although it posits an immortal soul. Orthodox Jews, by contrast, emphasize bodily resurrection, judgment of the soul, and immortality after resurrection. Conservative Jews retain belief in resurrection and immortality, while respecting wide latitude for verbally expressing these hopes.[2]

Compounding Jewish dialogue about death is the immense scope of violence Jews have experienced on account of their religious faith over the ages, largely at the hands of their Christian counterparts who erroneously blamed Jews for the death of Jesus. The crucible of religious persecution has contributed to Judaism's persistent tradition of questioning life's meaning in the light of suffering. The inquisitive posture of searching God for answers, once again, reflects the intimacy of a relationship between spouses. Even more important than arriving at sensible answers is the fact that Judaism has continued to pose the questions of meaning of life in the face of apparent meaninglessness and unbounded suffering. As Kramer puts it:

> The Jewish tradition is not of one accord theologically. In fact, Judaism contains a range of beliefs, from no view of an afterlife to a belief in the resurrection of the body and the immortality of the soul. Yet deeper than these seeming differences is a continued search for meaning despite life's absurdities. Indeed what could be more absurd than the Nazi concentration camps during the Second World War and the mass extermination of six million Jews? The question this nightmare raised was, and is: How could a just and loving God allow such inhumane atrocity to occur? On a different scale, this was also Job's question to God: Why am I, a righteous man, caused to suffer? And the answer given by God – "Where were you when I created the world?" – does not fully satisfy the question which is asked anew by each generation. But for the Jew, what is important is not so much the answer, but the search for meaning in life, one which offers no easy or completely satisfying answers.[3]

Since Judaism values tradition, continuity and life, its focus in death shifts to the bereaved. Jewish rituals for burial and mourning thus center around what will best help the living. It is customary for Jews to observe certain prescribed burial and structured mourning practices in order to refocus the energy of survivors toward reintegration in life rather than dwelling indefinitely in loss.

Rabbi Grollman details the process of traditional Jewish burial and mourning customs in the following way. The body of the deceased is washed, covered in a simple white shroud, and buried in a pine coffin. Someone stays with the body from death to interment. As the funeral begins, relatives of the deceased tear their garments or pin torn black ribbons to their clothes as a symbolic rending of their garments. The presiding rabbi recites traditional prayers, often drawn from the Book of Psalms, and offers a eulogy. Friends and family accompany the deceased to the cemetery for interment, and at the burial site, a

*Kaddish* (a prayer of condolence) is spoken. This begins the period called *Shiva*, which is an intensive seven-day time of mourning, during which the bereaved receive callers and visitors at their home. After the *Shiva*, the *Sh-loshim* begins, which is a thirty-day period marked by a resumption of regular activities but avoidance of recreation and entertainment. Except in the case of a parent, for whom mourning continues for a full year, regular life is resumed after thirty days. Each year, on the anniversary of the death, called the *Yahrzeit*, a *Kaddish* is spoken and a *Yahrzeit* candle is lit in memory of the deceased. These practices help to reaffirm the Jewish emphasis on life, while at the same time establishing an ongoing custom of remembering those who have died.[4] Grollman concludes, "Though reason cannot answer *why*, and the comforting words cannot wipe away tears, Judaism offers consolation in death by reaffirming life."[5]

### *Islam*

Like Judaism, Islam is a monotheistic religion rooted in the faith of Abraham. The religion began in 610 CE, when the Prophet Muhammad began receiving revelations from God, which his companions memorized and perfectly recorded. These revelations comprise the text of the Qu'ran, which Muslims believe to be the exact word of God, identified by the Arabic word Allah. Muslims hold this revelation to be the final and fullest revelation, begun in the Hebrew and Christian Bible and perfected in the Qu'ran. Islam understands God's revelation to have come through a successive line of prophets, including Abraham, Moses, and Jesus, and to have finally been completed in the Prophet Muhammad.

Initially located in Mecca in modern Saudi Arabia, Muhammad preached his monotheistic faith against a polytheistic culture that rejected his message. With his followers, the Prophet Muhammad was persecuted and eventually left for the city of Medina. During this period in Medina, however, the Prophet's movement gained tremendous support from followers with whom he established political, military, and religious authority. Between 622, when he originally fled to Medina, and his death in 632, the Prophet was able to unite the surrounding Arab tribes, re-conquer Mecca, and establish a religion that today is represented worldwide by over one billion adherents in three major denominations: Suni, Shia, and Sufi.

Derived from Islam's principal belief in the absolute oneness of God, Muslims understand the whole of human life as oriented around an essential unity of origin, purpose, and destiny in relationship to God. This understanding applies both to the individual human person and also to the entire Islamic community and the world at large. The Islamic understanding of human life, suffering, and dying, then, are intimately related to the Islamic understanding of God's absolute singleness, God's power, and God's dominion over all creation. The Qu'ran teaches that God created the universe, and that God has absolute control over its affairs. Moreover, the Qu'ran (as well as the Hadith[6]) has an eschatological tradition that teaches God has ordained a history of time between the initial creation of the universe and its final judgment and disposition. Islamic eschatology posits a cosmic timeline in which: 1) God creates; 2) signs occur to signify the Hour that initiates the end of earthly existence; 3) the death of everything; 4) the resurrection and judgment of the resurrected; and finally 5) eternal life.

Within this cosmic plan, human life and death occur according to God's intention and design. Islam repeats the story of the creation of the human couple in the Garden. In the Islamic rendering of the story, however, the human couple is not permanently marked by a condition of irrecoverable sin thereafter. Rather, humans are given life in order to prepare for a final judgment and to earn ultimate consignment to paradise or damnation. "From the Muslim standpoint, death is a transition from this world to Eternity."[7] Death is not, therefore, inherently bad, evil, or a result of sin. In fact, God causes all death before the final time of resurrection, thereby framing death within the total creative and providential power of God. Since human life is ultimately lived for the purpose of its last judgment and disposition, Muslims strive to structure their lives around highest ethical conduct and religious observance in submission to God.

As Jane Idelman Smith and Yvonne Yazbeck Haddad observe in their work *The Islamic Understanding of Death and Resurrection*,[8] Islamic eschatological traditions about the Day of Judgment are very detailed and hence answer, in an anticipatory way, questions about what happens at the time of resurrection and thereafter. What the Qu'ran is less specific about, however, is what happens during the time between a person's death and the time of resurrection itself. Is there a soul that is self-aware, suffering, blissful, or cognizant of time during death and resurrection? Smith and Haddad suggest that here there is room for speculation, although the Hadith traditions describe belief in an intermediate state, called the *barzakh*, in which the deceased person is challenged by questioning and potential punishments.

These traditions hold that upon death, two angels, named Munkar and Nakir, question the deceased about his religious beliefs and understanding of the Prophet. If the individual answers as a faithful Muslim, he is afforded peace as he awaits the resurrection and judgment. If the individual answers otherwise, he is subjected to punishment by the angels as God deems fitting. Smith and Haddad note that the emphasis on punishment here must be understood in light of the Islamic belief in God's ultimate justice, and "while descriptive in effect, their function as a whole [is] didactic and homiletic, implementing the divine injunction to command the good and prohibit the evil."[9]

Suffering and dying in Islam make sense when interpreted as challenges to Muslims to orient themselves morally and faithfully in absolute submission to the unsearchable will of God. God is understood as at once merciful and also just, and so Islamic teaching posits both hope for salvation and also fear of the consequences of hypocrisy and faithlessness.

Islamic burial rites reflect the ultimate hope for resurrection.[10] In death, the individual repents of sin and speaks the Islamic creed, called the

*Shahada*: "There is no God but Allah, and Muhammad is his Prophet." If the dying person cannot speak, relatives recite the creed. The body is laid on its back, with the head facing Mecca. The body is prepared by cleansing and shrouding with a white cotton sheet. The deceased is placed in a simple wood coffin and carried to the burial site. After an imam recites traditional prayers, the body is buried and mourners cover it with dirt and flowers. The dirt symbolizes the dust from which God has created the human and from which God will again resurrect the deceased on the Day of Judgment.

## Abrahamic attitudes – summary and comparison

Judaism and Islam share some fundamental conceptions about God, human life, and the experience of death. In both systems, God is singular and the absolute power over the cosmos. God created the universe, and God's power is beyond full comprehension. The human is bound to live a moral life according to God's laws, and those laws have been revealed through the prophets. Death is a natural part of God's creation. For some Jewish believers, and for all Muslims, death is an antecedent to a final resurrection and judgment.

Judaism and Islam, however, differ in some key ways as well. For Jews, God's revelation does not extend to the revelation of Muhammad, and conversely Muslims thus see the Jewish prophetic tradition as incomplete. In addition, Islamic eschatology is more fleshed out than Jewish conceptions of the end. Therefore, Islam has a more concretized conception of death and afterlife than Judaism. While some schools of thought within Judaism posit open-ended questions about the meaning of suffering, Islam places that discussion squarely within its understanding of the absoluteness of God's sovereignty. On this point, orthodox Judaism and Islam may be quite similar. Islam also has a more descriptive conception of heaven and hell than Judaism posits.

Conceptions of death and afterlife in Judaism and Islam also bear similarities and dissimilarities to Christian thought. Of course, both share the story of sin in the Garden and attach the difficulties of human life to the human need for moral correction. Neither, however, embraces the notion of an original sin in humanity that required Jesus to remove as the messianic mediator. Moreover, while Islam embraces Jesus as a prophet, it rejects as polytheistic the Christian claim that Jesus is the Incarnation of God. Orthodox Judaism, Christianity, and Islam also share the notions of resurrection, judgment, and final recompense, but each has its own eschatology to describe how these final cosmic events will unfold. Indeed, it is in the area of eschatology that the religions might be most at odds with one another both doctrinally and also socio-politically.

## Eastern traditions: Hinduism, Buddhism, Taoism

The Eastern cultures have a deep and rich history of reflecting on the meaning of human life, its suffering, and the fear that accompanies the inevitability of death. The Eastern religions recognize the common human impulse to fear death as that which brings an end to personal, individual existence. They further recognize that negative emotions and ideas attached to death produce a host of spiritual, relational, psychological, and philosophical disturbances for the living. Unresolved fear of death distorts the ability to live joyfully, freely, and in ways keeping with the true nature of existence. Thus, the Eastern religious and philosophical traditions have cultivated for thousands of years teachings, spiritual disciplines, and attitudes that help to reframe death as an integral and liberating stage in the cosmic processes of life.

The Eastern traditions understand liberation from death as related to intellectual and spiritual enlightenment while living. This enlightenment involves the mind disciplining itself to discover the authentic nature of its being. Eastern traditions identify individual existence as illusory insofar as people problematically mistake it for a permanent or fixed reality. By contrast, Eastern thought stresses the impermanence of all individual lives, which are understood as fleeting aggregates of physical and mental energies. When one comes to understand individual, personal life in its impermanence, one recognizes the error of overattachment to things and persons that are themselves always in the process of dissolution. One further recognizes that in their dissolution, individuals are not destroyed but rather participate in a greater cosmic process. Therefore, the self, when it understands its true nature, comes to recognize itself as a manifestation of these very cosmic processes, as inseparably one with them. Death, then, comes to be seen as not really death at all, but a return and reintegration into the greater whole. These basic ideas are fleshed out specifically in several distinct schools of thought, including: Hinduism, Buddhism, and Taoism.

### *Hinduism*

Hinduism is one of the earliest world religions, with sources dating to six thousand BCE. The name derives from the Indus River in India, but Hindus call their religion the *Sanatana dharma*, meaning the "eternal tradition." While having its origins in India, over nine hundred million Hindus are found throughout the world today. The goal of Hindu faith is to instruct human consciousness in understanding that the true nature of all life is an aspect of the eternal reality, known as *Brahman*.

The term *Brahman* refers to ultimate reality, which may be personified in the three divine beings of Brahma, Vishnu, and Shiva. Brahma, Vishnu, and Shiva represent respectively the ultimate and cyclical powers of the creation, sustenance, and destruction of the universe. Moreover, these personifications of *Brahman* can interact directly with humanity in the form of avatars such as Rama or Krishna. Hinduism is non-exclusive of other religions, so its adherents may also meaningfully seek spiritual edification in other religious traditions. Hinduism has multiple spiritual practices that help train the body and mind to experience the illumination of the consciousness, including scholarly study and yogic meditations. Hindus also have several holy or sacred books, including the Vedas, the Epics, and the Tantric literature. In varying genres, these texts teach the basic Hindu truths about the meaning and nature of life.

As with every religious tradition, the Hindu attitude toward suffering and dying is attached to its fundamental understanding of life. In Hinduism, the innermost soul, called the *atman*, is striving to achieve union with the ultimate reality of *Brahman*. In order to do this, it must achieve liberation, called *moksha*, from the cycle of death and reincarnation, called *samsara*. The *atman* is bound to *samsara* when past actions and wrong ideas preclude the soul from achieving union with *Brahman* upon death. This effect is known as *karma*. In Hinduism, time is understood as cyclical and endless, so all souls will eventually work through their *karma* and achieve liberation, just as all souls will eventually reinter the lifecycle.

Suffering and death are part of this cyclical process. Suffering is an aspect of *karma*, and it has a purifying effect on future incarnations. Moreover, life and death together must be understood as part of the cyclical process of universal life. All aspects of life are manifestations or aspects of *Brahman*, and all individuals are eventually destined to be restored in an undifferentiated way with *Brahman*. As a result, just as the personal permanence is a faulty concept, so also is ultimate death a faulty concept. Although discreet personal incarnations pass away, all life is eternal and connected in the reality of *Brahman*. The challenge in human life, then, is to come to understand this and to recognize *oneself as Brahman*. When this is achieved, fear of death evaporates. As Kenneth Kramer succinctly puts it, "Death therefore is natural and unavoidable. But it is not real. Only union with Brahman is real."[11]

### *Buddhism*

Buddhism is a reform movement of the Hindu tradition described above. It was begun by Siddhartha Gautama in the sixth century BCE. Born the prince of a petty kingdom, Siddhartha's early life was characterized by splendor and leisure. As a young man, he sought information beyond the sheltered limits of his upbringing and eventually left his kingdom's walls, where he encountered for the first time in his life poverty, sickness, old age, and death. Shocked by these hardships, Siddhartha set out on a quest to end suffering. As he pursued this goal, he spent many years as an ascetic yogi, until realizing that enlightenment would be found in a more moderate approach, known as the Middle Way. Legend has it that upon leaving the ascetic life, Siddhartha committed to sit in meditation under a Bohdi tree until he found the answer to end suffering. After weeks of meditation, he experienced enlightenment in the form of the Four Noble Truths. For Siddhartha, these truths provided the answer to end human suffering.

The first of these truths is that all life is suffering. The nature of existence, from birth to death, is fraught with pain. What is more, the cycle of reincarnation keeps people locked in a perpetual cycle of painful existence. The second truth is that all suffering is caused by ignorance of the nature of reality. Ignorance leads to craving, desire, and attachment to things that are inherently fleeting. The third truth is that suffering can be ended by the elimination of misbegotten attachments to impermanent things. Finally, the fourth truth is that attachments can be eliminated by following The Noble Eightfold Path. This path involves the disciplining of morality, wisdom, and concentration through the cultivation of: 1) right views; 2) right intention; 3) right speech; 4) right action; 5) right livelihood; 6) right effort; 7) right mindedness; and 8) right contemplation.

As a reform movement of Hinduism, Buddhism revises the concept of human life so as to suggest that there is in actuality no soul that needs to discover its true nature. Buddhism maintains that the human is not a soul but rather a composite of aggregates of material body, feelings, perceptions, *karma*, and consciousness. This is the teaching of *anatman*, which means "no soul." When one perceives a person, it is actually only a perception of fleeting aggregates that are in a perpetual state of flux. As such, a person is not a permanent reality. *Karma*, produced by individual actions and choices, adds to the aggregate of consciousness and keeps people in a cycle of incarnation. This does not indicate a permanence of soul but merely a continuation of contingent aggregates. When enlightenment, called *Nirvana,* is achieved, the Buddhist is finally released from the life–death cycle and suffering.

The impact on attitudes toward suffering and dying is great. For the Buddhist, suffering is expected in life to the extent that humans are attached to people, things, themselves, and so on. To understand something in its impermanence, by contrast, is liberating because one recognizes that the thing he desired was not real to begin with. A strategy of right knowledge and right living ensues, whereby anxiety and anticipatory grief over death are overcome.

Buddhists cultivate a variety of meditative habits related to different schools of thought, including the distinct expressions of Zen and Tibetan Buddhism. Zen Buddhism, predominant in Japan, emphasizes the importance of meditation toward the goal of achieving an enlightened state of consciousness. This state of consciousness, called *satori*, is an ineffable state in which the mind transcends the normal categories of rational knowing and recognizes the nondualistic nature of all being. Death and life are inherently related and simultaneously co-existing. Havelka attempts a description as follows:

> We shouldn't think of it as a state of quietude only, or a passive tranquilization, but as an inner awareness that has a unique noetic quality of consciousness. Such a consciousness goes beyond any ordinary categorization; it is both an understanding of any object and at the same time it reveals its deepest meaning beyond any classification. A distinct sense of "beyond" is present in Satori; one might call it God, Godhead, the Absolute and yet none of these terms conveys the essence of such an experience.
>
> This quality of Self-realized awareness is a most sublime psychological state that captures any moment as carrying an imprint of death. It

> "eternalizes" every distinct moment and opens a radically new view of life constantly linked with its polarity, death. Thus death mingles with every moment of life and while it underscores its impermanency, it begins to lose finality.[12]

Beyond others, Tibetan Buddhism has made a formal practice of contemplating and preparing its adherents for death. This form of Buddhism is part of the Vajrayana tradition, which orients its followers to entertain the experience of death during life so as to be prepared properly for death when it actually happens. These Buddhists teach and recite the *Bardo Thodol*, the *Tibetan Book of the Dead*, toward this end.

The *Tibetan Book of the Dead* is aimed at cultivating in the dying person the right disposition to encounter death so that good *karma* will be maximized and bad *karma* minimized, ensuring either a good subsequent incarnation and, ideally, liberation itself. The text deals directly with the intermediate experiences that come between death and rebirth, including: the visions that may accompany the mediate realm between life and liberation; guidance for entering the Buddha-realm; and instructions for selecting an appropriate womb for reincarnation. Tibetans study this text in life, read it as they directly prepare for death, and read it aloud to the body of the recently deceased based on the belief that the soul does not immediately detach from the body. The value and purpose of the *Bhardo Thodol* for Tibetans is neatly summarized in its concluding passage, which reads:

> [O]ne should approach all who have died, and if the corpse is present, a friend should read this reminder again and again ... In the presence of the corpse friends and relations should not weep and mourn and make noise, which may be done elsewhere; and as many acts of virtue as possible should be done ... One should read this continually and learn the word-meanings and terms by heart; then when death is certain and the signs of death have been recognized, if one's condition allows one should read it aloud oneself and contemplate it, and if one is not able to do that it should be given to a dharma-brother to read, for this reminder will certainly liberate, there is no doubt. This teaching does not need any practice, it is a profound instruction which liberates just by being seen and heard and read. This profound instruction leads great sinners on the secret path ... Even if the buddhas of the past and present and future were to search, they would not find a better teaching than this.[13]

## *Taoism*

Taoism is a Chinese philosophical and religious system, influenced by Buddhism, that dates from about the fourth century BCE. Among Chinese schools of thought, Taoism is comparable to Confucianism in scope and influence. The principal Taoist teachings can be found in the *Tao-te Ching*, a text that teaches about "the Way." This text is attributed to the fifth-century-BCE historical figure Lao-Tzu. Whereas Confucianism is mainly concerned with the preservation and perfection of standards for an ideal social system, Taoism focuses on the underlying patterns of universal energies, known as "the Tao" or "the Way." The goal of Taoism is to attune the individual to living without struggle in compliance with the universal Tao.

To be aligned with the Tao, one has to "do nothing" (*wuwei*). Doing nothing means to refrain from unnatural or strained actions that go against one's fundamental nature. To follow the Tao requires people to "unlearn" doctrines, systems, patterns, and so on, that produce an artificial construct of both self and the world. In the emptying process, one is able to transcend all artificial distinctions, such as the essential distinction between life and death.

As the universe is constantly in a state of flux, the Tao may be thought of as the process of endless transformation between states of being. Human life, like all life, is an aspect of endless interaction of complementary opposites. The Taoist symbol of the yin and yang visually represents the continuous flux in all nature. This flux is neither good nor bad; it is simply the Way of things. However, human beings have the ability to joyfully observe and appreciate this process, when we understand the limits and nature of human life within the cosmic processes. Kramer describes this process in the following passage:

> Beyond all human change, nature continues to express itself within never-ending cycles of transformation. Waves swell and fall from the horizon flowing to the lap of the beach, finally to crash and dissipate into white froth, only to return to the sea beneath the next wave. So, too, human life terminates with a reversal of direction, from oncoming to outgoing, from Yang to Yin.[14]

## Eastern attitudes – summary and comparison

The Eastern traditions vary in some specific ways, but each strives to instruct individuals in how to integrate death as a natural aspect within the overall experience of life. Death is not a foreign invasion into life or an inversion of what is essentially natural. Pain, suffering, and grief may be minimized by reforming intellectual and emotional attitudes toward our own selves in light of: 1) the truly impermanent nature of individual existence; and 2) the truly eternal nature of being itself from which individual existences come and to which they invariably return.

In the actual dying process, Eastern traditions may emphasize formal and ritualized patterns of mourning; meditative practices; chanting; restraint in public expressions of fear and grief; and concern for maximizing the conditions and atmosphere conducive to a dignified and focused death. To approach death with quietude is to die honorably and in accordance with the nature of things. Far from being an indicator of apathy on the part of the dying or the bereaved, calm is necessary for the dying person to achieve liberation or a desirable reincarnation. Crying and outward shows of emotion could cloud entrance into the next stage of being. Death in Eastern cultures may be accompanied by some specific needs, such as the lighting of incense, the presentation of an icon for meditation, or making preparation for returning bodily remains to an ancestral home.

Although there are some obvious outward distinctions between Christian conceptions of life and death and the Eastern attitudes, there are also some interesting points of overlap. Among the most significant distinctions are the conceptualization of God and the nature of divine–human interaction. In the Christian model, God is highly personified, and interacts with people in very intimate ways. In the most intimate of ways, God becomes human in the person of Jesus. In the Eastern models, the doctrine of God is far more effusive. The Buddhist concept of *Nirvana* and the Taoist concept of the Way are both non-conceptual and non-personified. The Hindu concept of *Brahman* is perhaps closest to the Christian model insofar as it posits three aspects of God (which could be likened to the three persons of the Christian Trinity). However, *Brahman* is at last ineffable and encompassing of all things, while the Christian doctrine of God retains an ultimate distinction between God and the created universe.

A second important distinction is the origin of suffering and death. In the Christian theological system, suffering and death result from human disobedience to God. Humans were intended to live a paradisiacal existence, but lost this blessing through a poor exercise of free will. Suffering is attached to sin and personal responsibility. In the person of Jesus, suffering becomes redemptive, creating the spiritual practices that tolerate (if not celebrate) suffering as a corrective vehicle for moral corruption. In the Eastern models, by contrast, suffering and dying are not directly derived from sin nor construed as punishment for human error. They are merely part of the cycle of life. Suffering, like everything else, is fleeting. And, just as life is illusory, so is death. Sin and error are corrected not by a mediator such as Jesus, but rather through the working out of *karma* in successive incarnations.

There are many relevant commonalities that could be identified, but two particularly salient to this discussion are: 1) the concern to ease human suffering; and 2) the emphasis on life beyond death. In both the Christian and Eastern traditions here considered, the major spiritual thrust is on easing the spiritual burdens caused by suffering and dying. The religious figures such as Jesus, the Hindu avatars, Buddha, and Lao-Tzu teach lessons about compassion, self-understanding, and the integral relationship between living well and dying well. Each of these traditions cultivated spiritual practices and disciplines aimed at training disciples in healthy attitudes toward dying, both for their own edification and also so that they could teach others through their words and examples. Moreover, the comforting message these visionaries taught was that death is not the end of life but the occasion of a new birth. In the Christian model, that new birth is framed in terms of Jesus' Resurrection and eternal life with

God. In the Eastern models, it is framed in terms of literal new birth in reincarnation or as reintegration with ultimate reality itself. Though the concepts are distinct, they share the common lesson that life persists beyond death.

## Conclusion

A comparative consideration of suffering and dying reveals a range of differences among belief systems as well as significant commonalities. Being aware of a variety of perspectives helps us to be sensitive to one another in today's religiously plural world, and it also shows us some timeless and cross-cultural features of the human experience of suffering and loss:

1. People have a perennial need to try to make sense of suffering and loss. The way in which suffering is understood is directly related to a religious system's overall understanding of the origin, purpose, and destiny of human life.
2. Religious thought on suffering and dying is not absolute. Even highly descriptive systems of belief about death and afterlife cannot speak unquestionably and definitively about what happens after death.
3. Suffering is often understood as an opportunity for moral, intellectual, and spiritual growth and illumination.
4. Religious belief systems posit some existence that extends beyond the end of individual human life. Such belief may be as specific to personal existence as individual resurrection, or it may be as general as return to the cosmic processes of life itself. In both cases, comfort and hope are attached to the possibility of life beyond death.
5. The attitude toward death shapes both the funerary and burial rites as well as the nature of mourning and spiritual care for the bereaved.

Religious thought on suffering and dying across the spectrum constitutes the theological aspect of a person's (or a community's) experience of suffering and dying. While the theological framework is critical to faith, this framework must be complemented by good models of care that deal with needs beyond the intellectual grappling with death. It is to these issues that we now turn.

## Questions for review and discussion

1. Recount the experiences you have of individuals with different religious beliefs than yours. Have you discussed differences in religious belief? If yes, what is the experience like?
2. Is it helpful to learn about religious attitudes toward death that are different from those you hold? Why or why not?
3. Can you identify common themes in all the religious beliefs considered in this chapter? If so, what are they?

4 What are the major differences you see in Abrahamic and Eastern thought patterns on suffering and dying?
5 Does your place of employment support and respect diversity of religious belief and practice? In what ways? How could it be more supportive?

## Resources

Doka, Kenneth J. and John D. Morgan, Eds. *Death and Spirituality*. Amityville, New York: Baywood Publishing, 1993.

Donovan, Jean. *The Mystery of Death: Reflections on the Spiritual Tradition*. New York and Mahwah, New Jersey: Paulist Press, 1991.

Hopfe, Lewis M. and Mark R. Woodward. *Religions of the World*, Twelfth Edition. Upper Saddle River, New Jersey: Pearson, 2012.

Kramer, Kenneth. *The Sacred Art of Dying*. Mahwah, New Jersey: Paulist Press, 1988.

Morgan, John D., Ed. *Readings in Thanatology*. Amityville, New York: Baywood Publishing, 1997.

# 7 Issues in spiritual caregiving for the suffering and dying

> There is no society without worshipers,
> There is no time without someone who prays.
> There is no place that cannot be transformed into a place of prayer
> And there is no human being who does not, in the privacy of his heart, embrace a silent prayer, offered up to the hidden powers, to redeem him from his distress,
> To improve his condition and to better his lot.
> The human being is a being who prays.
>
> David Weiss Halivni[1]

## Introduction

The opening reflection of this chapter, written by David Weiss Halivni, comes from his essay entitled "Prayer in the Shoah." In this essay, Halivni reflects upon the nature of prayer in the Nazi labor camps. In his reflection, Halivni is tasked to explore two basic aspects of spiritual life in the Holocaust. In the first, by a close consideration of the Hebrew law, prophets, and writings, Halivni argues stringently against those who might suggest that the Holocaust may be interpreted as God's punishment of the Jewish people for some error on their behalf. Such a suggestion, Halivni contends, places blame upon the six million Jewish victims of the Nazis and makes their murderers God's agents. The second task, however, derives from the first. Halivni must consider the correlating question of *why*, if this were not God's will, *why God would allow this to happen*? Why did God not, as in the time of the exodus, intervene to stop this evil that led to the senseless loss of so many lives? It is here where Halivni probes the enigma of prayer in the Shoah and where, I think, Halivni sheds light on how this enigma is broadly emblematic of all human struggle and response to suffering. In the face of unprecedented cruelty and the attempted (and largely realized) murder of an *entire* people, prayer was still possible for Halivni and the others with him who were destined for suffering and death. As the interred Jews prayed for God to "rule over all," they expressed the essential human hope that God would be God; that justice would prevail; and that their suffering would be redeemed. As his opening words here intimate, even when it was unclear whether and by whom the prayer would ever be heard or addressed, the human continued to pray, to endure, and to make sense of the ordeals ultimately and inevitably and only in the depths of prayer.

Prayer arises from suffering and coexists alongside the theological questions of why people must suffer and whether suffering has any meaning. In many religious schools of thought, paradisiacal existence (either before birth or after death) is posited as a real alternative to finite, creaturely life. Yet, within finite, creaturely existence, pain and death are inevitable. One cannot avoid some measure of pain in life, and no one escapes the cessation of biological functioning that is called *death*. Everyone is thus tested with the spiritual question of death.

The attitudes with which people suffer, die, and grieve, however, give the color, texture, and meaning to their experiences of pain and death. Through their various modes of prayer and spiritual practice, people are not consigned to endure suffering passively; they may also be active participants in how they deal with suffering and death. One is here reminded of Viktor Frankl's courageous answer to the suffering he endured in those same camps:

> What was really needed was a fundamental change in our attitude toward life. We had to learn ourselves and, furthermore, we had to teach despairing men, that it did not really matter what we expected from life, but rather what life expected from us. We needed to stop asking about the meaning of life, and instead to think of ourselves as those who were being questioned by life – daily and hourly. Our answer must consist, not in talk and meditation, but in right action and in right conduct. Life ultimately means taking the responsibility to find the right answer to its problems and to fulfill the tasks which it constantly sets for each individual ... When a man finds that it is his destiny to suffer, he will have to accept his suffering as his task; his single and unique task. He will have to acknowledge the fact that even in suffering he is unique and alone in the universe. No one can relieve him of his suffering or suffer in his place. His unique opportunity lies in the way in which he bears his burden.[2]

Even under the worst imaginable circumstances, suffering and dying have potential to become a concluding stage of learning, wisdom, and growth in the human life. This is not meant to suggest that suffering and death ought, therefore, to be pursued or celebrated as goods in their own right (especially in such scope as the Shoah). It is to suggest, however, that both suffering and dying may occasion unexpected opportunities for growth, personal spiritual insight, the attainment of wisdom, and the potential to teach invaluable lessons to the living.

Human beings, regardless of belief or creed, share the inevitability of death with one another. Everyone loses loved ones, and everyone stands to leave others behind in their own passing. This reality means that, while some people make caregiving a profession, all people have a vocation to care for others as well as themselves in illness, death, and bereavement. Yet, despite the universality of the call to caregiving, one of the greatest challenges in modern society remains lack of skill and language to deal with death. Especially in the first world, advances in medical technology have removed death from the immediacy of home and relocated the dying to institutional settings. Whereas death is a natural limit to human life, the medical sanitization of death has reframed it as an unnatural intrusion or interruption. Joan Halifax speaks to this modern phenomenon:

> Many of us today have lost a vital connection to the life cycle of birth and death, increasingly cut off as we are from traditional community and extended family. In previous centuries, it would have been unlikely that anyone would have reached adulthood without being present at the bedside of one or more deaths, and as a result our forebears might have had a healthier view of dying as the natural end to life.[3]

Compounding this phenomenon is a profound emphasis on youth culture in popular media, which masks the aging process and its attendant potential for wisdom and maturity. Thus, today, perhaps more than in previous eras, people (professional and otherwise) are less equipped to deal with death holistically and constructively. As such, people today require a renewed skill set for facing their own mortality as well as that of others.

In the previous chapters, we considered theological responses to the human experience of suffering. In this chapter, we will now look at the ways in which that theological dialogue may be practically applied in the spiritual care of those enduring suffering and facing death. This represents a perspective shift to a focus on medical research, practitioner experience, and lessons in caregiving derived from end-of-life experts. This shift is intentional and represents the operating assumption of this book that suffering engages both: 1) the philosophical questions of meaning that theology attempts to respond to; and also 2) a practical need to engage suffering persons in concrete acts of compassionate care. To this end, we will consider: 1) recent developments in the field of thanatology; 2) a brief overview of special topics pertaining to spiritual care of the dying; and 3) a brief overview of special topics pertaining to spiritual care of the bereaved.

## Thanatology

Recognizing the need for better death education, researchers across a spectrum of disciplines have contributed to a growing field of studies called *thanatology* (death studies). These studies have repeatedly revealed that the experiences of suffering and dying are largely defined by spiritual concerns. In other words, spiritual concerns are at least as important as medical concerns for people facing serious illness. It is here necessary to note that "spiritual" concerns are not identical with "religious" concerns, although the two may significantly overlap. While religion deals explicitly with belief systems and worship practices, spirituality more broadly describes the whole spectrum of questions about meaning, purpose, hope, and despair. Awareness of these penetrating concerns is the first step in developing a healthy understanding of the impact suffering has on the heart and mind.

Much of the current research and study of the spiritual needs of dying patients comes from the modern hospice movement.[4] While the first hospices date to the eleventh century CE (for the care of crusaders and pilgrims who became terminally ill while journeying), the principles of hospice today derive largely from Dame Cicely Mary Saunders' work with St Luke's Home for the Dying Poor and St Christopher's Hospice, which she founded in 1967. Dame Saunders worked as a nurse and physician, and her experiences at the patient bedside led her into an acute awareness of the concept of "total pain," which Saunders believed involved the range of physical, psychological, spiritual, and relational (or familial) needs. Saunders strove to develop institutional models that could provide broad spectrum pain management aimed at providing expert medical care; family services; patient recreational opportunities and therapies; homecare resources; spiritual care; care for the caregivers; and even salon services for patients' hair maintenance. Saunders' holistic hospice philosophy[5] underlay the model of patient and family care at her founding institution of St Christopher's Hospice (where she herself died in 2005) and has spread throughout the past several decades to similar facilities in the United Kingdom, the United States, continental Europe, Canada, Japan, China, Russia, India, and Africa.

Coterminous with the work of Dame Saunders was the thanatology research of Swiss psychiatrist Elisabeth Kübler-Ross. Dr Kübler-Ross' work largely emerged from her time at the University of Chicago's Pritzker School of Medicine, where she incorporated interviews with dying patients into her medical lectures. Her techniques provided terminally ill individuals with an opportunity to voice their experiences, revealing the commonly inadequate attention paid to their holistic needs as persons and not just as patients. Based on her research, Kübler-Ross published the landmark text *On Death and Dying*,[6] in which she laid out her conceptual stages of human grieving and dying. These include: denial; anger; bargaining; depression; and acceptance. This model of grieving was designed to explain the common internal states that terminal patients experience (although Kübler-Ross noted that these stages are not necessarily sequential; experienced by everyone; of equal duration in length; or transcended permanently once experienced). Kübler-Ross later suggested that the stages of grief were also experienced by persons undergoing other types of losses and traumas as well (such as divorce, job loss, or surviving the death of a loved one). Today, some researchers dispute the Kübler-Ross model of the stages of grief, but her work remains deeply impactful in raising understanding of the depth and scope of psychological suffering that accompanies physical illness and impending death.

Contemporary researchers have been helpful in the continuing effort to refine and improve both the understanding and also the practice of spiritual caregiving to the dying. Patrice O'Connor's work,[7] for example, identifies three principal spiritual concerns that surface when people suffer, especially during serious illness and at end of life. These include: spiritual issues; spiritual needs; and spiritual pain. *Spiritual issues* involve the range of past history and faith questions that a person has not previously addressed but which surface during illness. Such issues can include: unresolved relationships; unresolved conflicts with intimates; religious questions that have not been satisfactorily answered; past issues with pastors or religious educators; and so on. *Spiritual needs* are the specific needs a person has which can be met by direct actions. Such needs include, for example, contacting pastors or priests for consultations, sacraments, anointing, and so on; having a pet brought by for a visit; being taken outside for a walk; having a window in one's room so as to see natural light; having access to drawing paper and pencils; and so on. Spiritual needs can often be ascertained simply by asking someone straightforwardly what is needed, what brings a sense of comfort, and what nourishes the individual's spirit (which may or may not be religious in nature). *Spiritual pain* refers to the spectrum of psycho-social and existential concerns that surface in the transition from vitality to impending mortality. Spiritual pain typically extends beyond the individual who is suffering and encompasses the web of family and friends who define a person's most intimate human relationships.

Richard Groves and Henriette Anne Klauser, based on over twenty years of combined work with dying persons, further refine the concept of spiritual pain in their work *The American Book of Dying*.[8] Here, using case studies to illustrate these issues, they identify four key aspects to spiritual pain that surface across culture and time, regardless of religious faith or creed. These include: meaning pain; hopelessness pain; relationship pain; and forgiveness pain. *Meaning pain* is pain over what happens to the value and purpose of life when an individual can no longer fulfill the same meaning socially and relationally as she or he did in the prime of life. For example, if one had a successful career but can no longer act in a professional capacity, a sense of loss over the past and confusion over the relevance of one's present state can produce a crisis of meaning. *Hopelessness pain* refers to the pain that emerges when hope for recovery and return to health dissipates. Although hope is possible in all stages of life, for those who suffer, especially at the end of life, hope must be redefined and calibrated to different expectations (such as hoping for a good day rather than hoping for a cure). Transitioning in stages of hope can produce a sense of loss and despair, especially when an individual has difficulty redefining hope in ways appropriate to declining physical condition. *Relationship pain* refers to the pain associated with the anticipation of severing and the inevitable loss of relationships caused by death. A mother, for example, grieves over what will happen to her children without her to parent them. A spouse, as another example, grieves over the thought that someone else may take his role in a new marriage contracted after his death. *Forgiveness pain* refers to the pain associated with relationship and personal failures in life. At the end of life, it is often sorrow over what was and was not done, with and for and by, the ones we loved that produces the greatest obstacles to peace. Reconciling with oneself, one's loved ones, as well as with God (however God is defined for an individual), is the ultimate challenge of forgiveness.

Groves and Klauser further relate their findings about spiritual pain to a broader framework of wisdom on dying (and its lessons for the living) derived from world literary resources, such as *The Egyptian Book of the Dead*, *The Gnostic Books for the Living and Dying*, *The Tibetan Book of the Dead*, *The Celtic Books of the Dead*, and *The Monastic Books of the Dying*. Their survey of this literature surfaces seven common spiritual lessons at end of life that have been variously documented and attested throughout the breadth of recorded human experience. These include:

1. It is a priority that human beings assist each other as coaches or midwives through the stages of dying.
2. There are certain observable and universal patterns or stages in the life-to-death transition process.
3. There is a clear relationship between physical and emotional pain.
4. It is necessary first to diagnose spiritual pain before attempting to respond to it.
5. A "good death" is defined as our ability to maintain a sense of clear knowing or consciousness at the end of life.
6. Some form of consciousness survives the death of our physical body.
7. We prepare throughout our lifetime for our dying.[9]

All these researchers, and others like them, have come to articulate some essential truths about the processes of suffering and dying. At a bodily level, dying is accompanied by defined physical processes, many of which are well documented, such as in the case of the death occasioned by pathologies whose progressions are well understood and commonly encountered in the medical professions. Caregivers can, and indeed must, attend to physical treatments of illness, suffering, and pain (whether it be toward the aim of restoration or palliation). On a spiritual level, however, death itself becomes much more than physical processes against which we rally with medicines and hoped-for cures. Death is rather the font of the deepest dialogue with and insight into the essential dimensions of spirituality: love, trust, belief, forgiveness, hope, meaning, and relationship. To the extent that people cultivate within ourselves the capacity to think and speak about death, we can be present to others in our care as they themselves encounter death. Moreover, people can be present to ourselves in a more honest way that allows the inescapable fact of our own mortality to become both friend and guide to us concerning the manner in which we live and value. Again, Joan Halifax poignantly summarizes this point:

> In being with dying, we arrive at the natural crucible of what it means to love and be loved. In this burning fire we test our practices of not-knowing,

> bearing witness, and compassionate action, practices that can also hold us up through the most intense flames. Please, let us not lose our precious opportunity to show up for this great matter – indeed, *the only matter* – the awesome matter of life and death.[10]

## Spiritual care for the dying

Death presents spiritual challenges to both the dying and those they leave behind. As hospice nurses Maggie Callanan and Patricia Kelley observe in the opening of their work *Final Gifts*:

> A terminal illness doesn't belong only to the one who is sick – it affects family members, friends, neighbors, coworkers. Not unlike a still pond disturbed by a falling stone, an impending death sends ripples through all the relationships in the life of the dying. Each person involved has his or her own set of issues, fears, and questions.[11]

What is more, the experience of suffering and impending death differ based on the specific circumstances that accompany the suffering and dying. The following is a list of considerations that may impact, for better and for worse, individual experiences of death. Dealing with practical matters in a straightforward and directed fashion can create a better frame of mind in the dying person to focus on critical spiritual issues and personal relationship needs.

### *1 Legal issues*

Legal issues related to dying may not at first blush seem spiritual in nature, but in fact they overlap with a range of matters involving religious belief and practice; moral reasoning; and family and relationship issues. A patient, for example, may hold religious beliefs that would preclude her from receiving a medical intervention. If her family does not know or share her religious beliefs, and the patient cannot speak for herself, the patient's spiritual wellbeing and her family relationships may be compromised. The legal issues surrounding sickness and death are broad, including: estate planning and/or wills; advance funerary planning; medical and financial powers-of-attorney; advance directives for medical care; living wills; and ethical and legal issues surrounding the use and termination of life-sustaining medical interventions (such as nutrition; hydration; respiration; and resuscitation) and physician-assisted suicide. It is in the best interest of patients, medical caregivers, and family members to facilitate open discussion and advance planning surrounding patient and family expectations concerning the nature, duration, and termination of medical interventions. It is, further, in the best interest of patients and family members, wherever appropriate, to have conversation about estate planning and personal (and/or religious) intentions for funeral and burial. Advance planning can ease the dying person's concerns about "what will happen" and "who will be burdened," in addition to staving off family feuds over matters of medical care; inheritance; and funeral/burial preferences.

Resources to consider here include: Norman Cantor's *Advance Directives and the Pursuit of Death with Dignity* (Bloomington, Indiana: Indiana University Press, 1993); Nancy King's *Making Sense of Advance Directives* (Washington: Georgetown University Press, 1996); David DeGrazia's *Human Identity and Bioethics* (Cambridge and New York: Cambridge University Press, 2005); Debbie S. Bitticks, et al., *The Senior Organizer* (Deerfield Beach, Florida: Human Communications, Inc., 2006); and Joshua Slocum and Lisa Carlson's *Final Rights: Reclaiming the American Way of Death* (Hinesburg, Vermont: Upper Access, Inc., Book Publishers, 2011).

### *II Religious/spirituality assessment*

Suffering persons, especially at the end of life, experience intensified physical pain when spiritual and religious issues are inadequately addressed. In order to address and treat spiritual pain, caregivers (whether professional or personal) need to know what an individual's spiritual pains actually are. This information is acquired through the establishment of a trusting relationship between caregiver and patient in which open dialogue can occur. Soliciting spiritual information in a professional setting may occur during intake questionnaires or through the use of such tools, for example, as the FICA tool created by Dr Christina Puchalski of the George Washington Institute for Spirituality and Health. This brief spiritual inventory asks patients to describe: 1) **Faith** and belief; 2) **Importance** of faith and belief in overall health; 3) involvement in a religious or spiritual **Community**; and 4) how patients would like their spiritual needs to be **Addressed** in their care.[12] In more intimate settings, open and direct questions such as, "What brings you comfort?" and "Would you like me to bring someone in from the church/temple/mosque/etc. to be with you?" can be helpful. It is also important for caregivers to understand the religious faith of patients as well as possible, because aspects of faith frequently influence the actual medical care one receives as well as the disposition of body and bio-matter.

Helpful resources include Robert Kastenbaum's *The Psychology of Death*, Third Edition (New York: Springer Publishing Company, 2000); Jean Donovan's *The Mystery of Death: Reflections on the Spiritual Tradition* (Mahwah, New Jersey: Paulist Press, 2003); Robert M. Baird, Ed., and Stuart E. Rosenbaum's *Caring for the Dying: Critical Issues of the Edge of Life* (Amherst, New York: Prometheus Books, 2003); Gerald A. Larue's *Euthanasia and Religion: A Survey of the Attitudes of the World Religions to the Right-To-Die* (Los Angeles: Hemlock Press, 1985); and Maggie Callanan and Patricia Kelley's *Final Gifts: Understanding the Special Awareness, Needs, and Communications of the Dying* (New York: Bantam Books, 1997).

### *III Social location*

Social location is here defined as ethnic, economic, and gendered dimensions of a patient's demographic. An individual's social location shapes a variety of aspects that may affect or shape the death experience. Examples of such aspects include: attitudes and behaviors toward death held by an individual and his/her community; risk factors that make an individual more likely to experience certain types of illness or death (for example, genetic predispositions); family structures associated with social location; access (or lack thereof) to affordable medical care; risk factors associated with violence, incarceration, crime, and drug use that derive from systemic, economic community dysfunction; opportunities (or lack thereof) for education, recreation, and meaningful employment; the role of religious communities within the demographic; and so on. Social location impacts not only one's perception of death but also concrete aspects of the death experience.

One sees how social location may affect the death experience, for example, in the case study of death within the United States African-American community. Here one finds the following data:

1 black males have the highest death rates from accidents and violence than any statistical group;
2 suicide rates have risen at a faster rate for blacks than for whites;
3 infant mortality rates in the black community are double that of whites;
4 the odds of an African-American male being murdered are six times greater than for his white counterpart (eight times greater between the ages of 24 and 34);
5 a black female is three times more likely to be a homicide victim than her white counterpart; and
6 the survival rates (five-year survival rates) for most forms of cancer are significantly less for the black patient than for the population as a whole.[13]

Such sobering statistics reveal that economic and political realities place African-Americans at greater risk than the general population of violent and preventable deaths. As Meagher and Bell note, these factors extend beyond the experience of the dying and color the survivors' and community's experience of grief. "[D]eath that was preventable, one that is the result of a lack of money or a lack of available resources, has a very distinct effect on the bereavement process and on the attitudes and beliefs about life and death."[14]

Social location, of course, typically benefits the quality of the death experience for socially and economically dominant demographics. For vulnerable sets, however, their vulnerability translates ultimately into their experience of suffering and dying. Women worldwide represent perhaps the most vulnerable set. On the basis of their gender alone, for example, women are such frequent targets of intimate partner violence, sexual assault, and killing that the regularity of male violence against women is functionally accepted as a social norm.[15] In conflict zones, moreover, women (because they are women) are often targets of mass rape, enslavement, prostitution, forced abortion and sterilization, subjected to sexually transmitted diseases, and killed.[16] Even more, due to modern modes of communication and travel, women and girls have increasingly become targets for abduction, enslavement, pornography, prostitution, and slave labor in human trafficking rings.[17]

The vulnerability of women is compounded, furthermore, by ethnicity and low economic status, so that poor, minority women become the most vulnerable demographic in any society. These combined threats to women *as women* shape all women's overall sense of safety and wellbeing in their world as well as how women perceive God vis-à-vis their experiences of suffering. Here the range of works in feminist theology is helpful, as feminist authors explore not only women's vulnerability but also how that vulnerability has been, to a great extent, actually produced by religious concepts and structures that privilege men. Feminist theologians have discovered the use of religion as a tool of oppression against women, and thus attempt varyingly: 1) to devise alternate religious models that are not destructive of women; and/or 2) to recover and revision alternate interpretations of the classic religious systems that are not destructive to women.[18]

All liberation theologies are concerned with the interplay between suffering, death, and social location and are thus useful sources for considering the theological implications therein. Among many available treatments of death and social location written from ethics and practitioner perspectives, some helpful titles to consider here include: David Field, Ed., et al., *Death, Gender, and Ethnicity* (New York and London: Routledge, 1997); Richard A. Kalish and David K. Reynolds' *Death and Ethnicity: A Psychocultural Study* (Farmingdale, New York: Baywood Publishing, 1981); Suzanne Smith's *To Serve the Living: Funeral Directors and the African American Way of Death* (Cambridge, Mass.: Belknap Press, 2010); Kristine M. Rankka's *Women and the Value of Suffering: An Aw(e)ful Rowing Toward God* (Collegeville, Minnesota: Liturgical Press, 1998); and Ronald M. Green, Ed., et al., *Global Bioethics: Issues of Conscience for the Twenty-first Century* (New York and Oxford: Oxford University Press, 2008).

## *IV Manner of death*

The manner of death refers to the way a person actually dies. A key component to a good death, according to thanatology researchers, is empowering the dying person, as much as possible, to define how he or she dies. This involves, first and foremost, allowing a person at end of life to be maximally recognized as a full, autonomous personal agent. This involves, secondly, attempting however possible to allow a dying person to cultivate an atmosphere and experience that will be most conducive to his or her aesthetic and spiritual preferences. This may include the facilitation or limitation of visits with family and friends; the inclusion or exclusion of religious symbols, persons, and rites; the choice to be at home; the choice to use or not use medical interventions; and so on. Thanatology researchers further suggest that pain management and cognitive lucidity are essential to a good death, especially insofar as they allow an individual to act as an agent and to interact in a coherent and meaningful way with loved ones. David Kessler has articulated seventeen "rights" of the dying that significantly influence spiritual wellbeing, quality, and manner of death. These include:

1 The right to be treated as a living human being.
2 The right to maintain a sense of hopefulness, however changing its focus may be.
3 The right to be cared for by those who can maintain a sense of hopefulness, however changing this may be.
4 The right to express feelings and emotions about death in one's own way.
5 The right to participate in all decisions concerning one's care.
6 The right to be cared for by compassionate, sensitive, knowledgeable people who will attempt to understand one's needs.
7 The right to expect continuing medical care, even though the goals may change from "cure" to "comfort" goals.
8 The right to have all questions answered honestly and fully.
9 The right to seek spirituality.
10 The right to be free of physical pain.
11 The right to express feelings and emotions about pain in one's own way.
12 The right of children to participate.
13 The right to understand the process of death.
14 The right to die.
15 The right to die in peace and dignity.
16 The right not to die alone.
17 The right to expect that the sanctity of the body will be respected after death.[19]

In the famous, three-part Nightline interview series between Ted Koppel and former Brandeis University sociology professor Morrie Schwartz, Morrie (who is dying of Lou Gehrig's disease) shares with Ted his insight that everyone's manner of death will not be the same. Some people will strive for a peaceful death; others will strive for bravery. Some will strive for quiet; others will cling to anger. Morrie suggests that it is up to each person, and not one's caregivers, to arrive at the manner of death that is most suited to oneself. All manners of death are valid and not to be judged or compared to one another. Morrie then encourages his audience to find the manner of death best suited to oneself spiritually and to attempt to sustain it throughout the end of life. This, for Morrie, constitutes, in large measure, a good death.

Helpful resources for thinking about manner of death include: David Kessler, *The Rights of the Dying: A Companion for Life's Final Moments* (New York: HarperCollins Publishers, 1997); Verna Benner Carson and Harold G. Koenig,

*Spiritual Caregiving: Healthcare as a Ministry* (Philadelphia and London: Templeton Foundation Press, 2004); and the personal account of Morrie Schwartz's life captured in Mitch Albom's *Tuesdays with Morrie: An Old Man, A Young Man, and Life's Greatest Lesson* (New York: Doubleday, 1997).

## Spiritual care for the bereaved

Loss of a loved one through death (as well as other types of loss associated with, for example, work, employment, natural disaster, and so on) leaves survivors with challenges that they must negotiate over time. C. Murray Parkes describes these challenges as four: bereavement, grief, mourning, and religious faith.[20] Parkes defines *bereavement* as the situation that occurs when attachments are terminated. *Grief*, Parkes describes, as "the emotional reaction to loss. It results from bereavement, and because people can anticipate a loss, [grief] can precede [bereavement]."[21] Grief may thus be "anticipatory," and may be experienced by both a person who is dying, or threatened by illness, as well as by survivors. Parkes describes *mourning* as the way in which people publicly behave and manifest their grief. Mourning includes personal actions, displays of grief (such as crying), and rituals surrounding death, burial, and remembrance. Finally, Parkes describes *religious faith* as that which establishes context for understanding the meaning of death, the hope for that which comes after death, and the source for comfort and care for those who are bereaved.

Bereavement and grief can produce both spiritual crises and also spiritual opportunities for the bereaved. Loss tests constructed answers to life's meaning and challenges religious faith to hold up to the promises it makes. Kenneth Doka speaks to the blended effect of spirituality on bereavement in the following passage:

> Faith, with its rituals and beliefs, can be a powerful elixir at times of loss. Its rituals can provide structure and succor. Its beliefs may offer comfort and conciliation. Yet like many powerful tools, faith can have both constructive and destructive aspects. It may promise reunion and resurrection, yet also haunt the bereaved with fears of retribution and damnation. To some it may offer forgiveness, while in others it exacerbates guilt. Its rituals may comfort some and trouble others.
>
> But faith, whether in a theistic religious system or a philosophical system, is likely to be a part of the bereavement process. Just as dying has a spiritual dimension, so does death and bereavement. Questions about the value of the deceased's life, the meaningfulness of the survivor's existence in the face of loss, and the reason for death are common concerns in times of loss and have an inherently spiritual character.[22]

Doka goes on to describe a four-stage process in which spirituality intersects with the tasks of bereavement.[23] In the first instance, survivors have to "*accept the reality of the death*" of a loved one. Doka suggests that spiritual beliefs and religious rituals can serve as valuable tools in the initial stages of grief. It is here in particular that funerary rites and rituals play a powerful role. Howard Raether's research further suggests that grief can be eased if survivors play an active role in the arrangement and participation in public expressions of mourning. Raether thus refers to "funeral therapies."[24] In the second task of bereavement, Doka reports that the bereaved have to "*experience the pain of grief*." Religious faith and spirituality become dialogue partners with grief in this stage of bereavement, as survivors attempt to understand the meaning of loss and derive renewed sense of meaning and purpose for themselves after death.

In the third task, Doka relates that survivors need *"to adjust to an environment in which the deceased is missing."* And, in the final task, Doka shares that survivors need *"to emotionally relocate the deceased and move on with life."* For both of these tasks, religious belief can be an aid as well as a barrier. When survivors deal with issues of guilt, fear, and forgiveness, religion can act in service to both positive and negative experiences of bereavement. Here, plumbing the religious traditions for their wealth of resources can help survivors find workable answers to the most painful questions death raises.

While all bereavement intersects with issues of religious faith, theological belief, and spiritual practice, some experiences of bereavement are complicated further by special circumstances that interrupt our hopes for a "good death" or death that happens at an appropriate time and age. Such circumstances include death brought about by:

- AIDS
- suicide
- violent death and murder
- sudden death due to accident
- death brought about by drug use, overdose, or addiction
- perinatal death (including miscarriage, abortion, still birth, and neonatal mortality)
- maternal death
- death of a child
- children's grief over death of a parent or parents
- Alzheimer's disease
- death of loved ones in the military, police force, and emergency response fields
- death by natural disaster or epidemic

Untimely deaths, natural disasters, deaths that seem unfair and unnecessary, deaths of children and caregivers of young children – these all engage nearly bottomless questions about the meaning, order, and justice in the universe. They can lead to complicated spiritual struggles for those who survive and grieve, and thus special resources may be sought and employed in the wake of such spiritually devastating losses.

Resources to consider here include: Margaret S. Stroebe, Ed., et al., *Handbook of Bereavement: Theory, Research, and Intervention* (Cambridge and New York: Cambridge University Press, 1993); Betty Rolling Ferrell, *Suffering* (Sudbury, Mass.: Jones and Bartlett Publishers, 1996); James A. Fogarty, *The Magical Thoughts of Grieving Children: Treating Children with Complicated Mourning and Advice for Parents* (Amityville, New York: Baywood Publishing, 2000); Daniel Rudofossi, *Working with Traumatized Police Officer Patients* (Amityville, New York: Baywood Publishing, 2007); Nancy Boyd-Franklin, Ed., et al., *Children, Families, and HIV/AIDS: Psychosocial and Therapeutic Issues* (New York: Guilford Press, 1995); Charles A. Corr and David E. Balk, Eds, *Handbook of Adolescent Death and Bereavement* (New York: Springer, 1996); Charles A. Corr and David E. Balk, Eds, *Handbook of Childhood Death and Bereavement* (New York: Springer, 1996); and Sally S. Roach, *Healing and the Grief Process* (Albany, New York: Delmar, 1997).

## Conclusion

In the introduction to C. S. Lewis' book *The Problem of Pain*, Lewis offers a brief *apologia* for his work. He reveals that he was asked to write the book for a series and that he would have preferred to remain anonymous. For, it seemed ridiculous to Lewis that he himself should be perceived by anyone who knew him as claiming to be an expert on pain and death. Lewis felt competent to write about the theological tradition on suffering, but he recognized that there was a substantial gulf between the intellectual and the practical realities of suffering and dying. Lewis recognized that the higher task in dealing with the problem of pain is one of courage, patience, and compassionate care. Religious truths, divorced from concrete actions of care and kindness, are functionally useless. Indeed, one could argue that such truths would de facto become falsehoods. And yet, it is curiously religious truths that can bring the greatest comfort to people when they are first cared for in compassionate and concrete ways. Lewis neatly brings home this point when he says "[W]hen pain is to be borne, a little courage helps more than much knowledge, a little human sympathy more than much courage, and the least tincture of the love of God more than all."[25]

## Questions for review and discussion

1. Describe the modern-day field of thanatology. What areas of death research do you feel are lacking today? How might death research be more popularly disseminated?
2. Reflect on your own experiences of death. Have you observed in personal or professional experience good models of spiritual care? Why or why not?
3. Reflect on your own experiences of loss. What sorts of things were spiritual aids to you? What might have helped you better?
4. How would you describe a good death? Is there such a thing?

5 Describe your understanding of the challenge of social location and death. What sorts of things make death inequitable in the modern world?
6 Describe your understanding of complicated bereavement. Can you think of other circumstances than those mentioned in this chapter that would provide spiritual obstacles to bereavement? How might you address those obstacles to help someone who was grieving?

# 8 A toolbox for dealing with suffering and death

> Transformation toward the glory of God does not mean to defeat present existence or to revert to some original uncompromised state. Rather, it involves the reorientation and reconstruction of multiple dimensions of personal and shared life. The old language of conversion conveys this thoroughgoing transformation: it is conversion rather than evasion of our earthen situation and situatedness; it is being turned toward the grace and glory of God and turning toward greater integrity and richer relatedness with others and God.
>
> Kristine A. Culp[1]

The encounter between faith and suffering can provide opportunities for personal growth, compassionate action, and spiritual illumination, but the encounter is never easy. For most of us, thinking about death is scary and talking about it directly can be uncomfortable. One of the benefits of studying the theology of suffering is that this study can prepare people to deal with death in advance by equipping us with insight and resources that we can use when it is necessary. As Culp notes in the quote above, the human task is not to evade our circumstances. We could not do that even if we tried. The real task becomes to be renewed in our orientation to life itself, whatever it may bring. Culp describes the transformation toward embracing our circumstances as "conversion," and she suggests that such a turn is indelibly personal as well as communal.

For caregivers, it is particularly critical to be able to approach self and others honestly and as we actually are. Such an approach takes maturity and wisdom, challenging us to be comfortable in our own mortality and willing to be a companion to others as they encounter their own fundamental limits of health and life. In this challenging work, it is especially helpful to have a variety of tools to draw from, both to prepare for the encounter with suffering and also to employ in times of death and bereavement.

This chapter, then, is a collection of tools and resources for readers to use toward this preparation. The goal of presenting these tools is to provide suggested resources for further research, practice, study in the classroom, in personal processing, in professional teams, and in practical application with the suffering, dying, and bereaved. The tools presented here represent only a small sampling of the numerous and excellent resources currently available, and I encourage all students and teachers of this material to seek out additional resources that advance their study as well as to incorporate liberally into the learning process practical wisdom gained through professional experience and personal histories. Here I have organized tools into the categories of: creative writing and art tools; contemplative tools; film resources; and book resources.

## Creative writing and art tools

### *1 Spiritual inventory*

A spiritual inventory is a very useful tool that people can use in examining their perceptions and fears related to suffering and dying. It consists of responding to a series of questions about faith, self, and relationships with others. It is never too late or too early to inventory one's spiritual self. As Kathleen Dowling Singh notes, "A spiritual assessment is a helpful practice as we move close to dying. Such an assessment seems to arise naturally in the course of the profound psychological and spiritual transformations of dying."[2] Singh further observes that the questions people ask as they approach death, regardless of race and creed, tend to cycle around common themes and concerns. For people in the prime of life as well as for those at life's end, an honest assessment of our own responses to spiritual questioning is invaluable. The experience of taking a spiritual inventory can provide insight into ourselves that gives guidance and direction to how we choose to live out our lives in the time that we have, whether that time is measured in decades or in days. Singh suggests a number of key questions that helpfully guide the spiritual inventorying process. These include:

- Who have I been all this time?
- How have I used my gift of a human life?
- What do I need to "clear up" or "let go of" in order to be more peaceful?
- What gives my life meaning?
- For what am I grateful?
- What have I learned of life and how well have I learned to love?
- What have I learned about tenderness, vulnerability, intimacy and communion?
- How am I handling my suffering?
- What will give me strength as I die? What is my relationship with this which will give me strength as I die?
- If I remembered that my breaths were numbered, what would be my relationship to this breath right now?[3]

To these questions, others could be added, such as:

- Am I satisfied with my relationship with people close to me? If not, what might I be able to do to increase my satisfaction level with my relationships?

- Am I satisfied with my relationship to God/Higher Power/The Divine/my faith community, as I understand it? If not, what might I be able to do to increase my satisfaction with my relationship to God?
- Am I satisfied with my sense of self? If not, what might I be able to do to increase my satisfaction with my own self?
- Have I asked others for the help I might need in improving these relationships?
- Have I forgiven others, myself, and God for the disappointments in my life so that I can live and, when it is time, so that I can die freely and in peace?

There are many spiritual inventorying tools available. Some of these provide opportunities for detailed evaluation of the spiritual self in terms of participation in a specific faith tradition; lifestyle; physical wellbeing; psychological health; and so on. Many spiritual inventory tools are available online at little or no cost. Others are more extensively presented in book format. A simple internet search will surface a wealth of tools to choose from. After consulting available tools, in addition, it may also be helpful for caregivers to develop their own inventory questions in ways that make sense within the context of their own faith tradition, institutional settings, spiritual goals, and personal circumstances.

As a teacher, I use spiritual inventories with my students each semester and consistently, the experience of completing a spiritual inventory is among the most meaningful in the class. Students often remark that a spiritual inventory provides a safe opportunity to think about questions they might otherwise have avoided. They also remark on the value of taking time out of their busy schedules to "check in" with themselves spiritually and find that repeating the process annually is personally edifying.

### 2 *Journaling*

Journaling involves entering into a disciplined dialogue with oneself. Journaling can be freeform, where one writes about a broad range of thoughts and feelings that emerge over a period of time. It can also be directed, where one is tasked to write about specific subjects, thoughts, and experiences. In the tool chest offered by Richard F. Groves and Henriette Anne Klauser in their work *The American Book of Dying: Lessons in Healing Spiritual Pain*, they suggest a number of types of journaling exercises that may prove fruitful for persons contemplating suffering or facing death. These include: 1) recording drawing, and writing about dreams; 2) doing a life review; 3) mapping or "geographying" key moments in life in an effort to surface major themes, meaning, and points of personal transformation; 4) writing about prayer and meditative experiences; and 5) reflecting on sacred readings.

It may be especially helpful for an individual with limited physical capacity to have her words recorded for her by a trusted friend or to have video or audio recording replace the traditional format of the written journal. In any case,

Groves and Klauser suggest that, while journaling should be creatively approached without a sense of right or wrong methodology, the process should be treated with the highest respect and undertaken as a sacred act. This entails allowing for time to journal as one would to pray; finding a place to journal that is conducive to the sacredness of the endeavor; respecting the confidentiality of the journal; and using its contents only in the manner intended by the author.

### 3 *Art therapy*

Art therapy allows people to express themselves through visual media in nonverbal ways. In its professional sense, art therapy is a psychotherapeutic tool used by licensed psychologist-practitioners, who use art as the principal method of communication between the patient and the therapist. Art therapy is particularly effective because the visual media stand as a means of self-expression when words fall short of the task. Sometimes art therapy is employed by individuals who, through disability or impairment, are unable to express themselves verbally. For the dying, for those contemplating dying, or for caregivers, art media may be useful assets to assist in surfacing and expressing difficult emotions and feelings about death. In addition, art therapies may help people express and process their feelings about grief. Art therapies may, moreover, be especially useful to employ with children who are suffering or bereaved.

In ideal circumstances, a professional art therapist will be part of a caregiving team, for example, in a hospice setting or a counseling center. However, the absence of a licensed professional should not deter people from employing art to express themselves as they think about or anticipate death. Even more, one does not need to be an artist or to have honed art skills in order to participate in art therapy.

Art should be used as a liberating means of self-expression. For example, in my suffering and dying courses, I often ask students to sketch or draw their image or concept of God vis-à-vis human suffering. Some students return with simple sketches torn from spiral-bound notepads, while others bring in sophisticated drawings and paintings. Both the simple sketches and the amateur masterpieces serve the same purpose of helping students to convey their sense of the Divine. Sometimes students surprise themselves with the images they choose. Students have created images of hands, trees, families, planets, weeping figures, exalted figures, blank pages, collages of religious symbols, and more. When shared (electively) in class, the breadth of concepts becomes a powerful launching pad for discussion about the range of human experiences of God and the depth of the human experience of suffering.

### 4 *Music therapy*

The human body is primordially rhythmical. In utero, babies gestate to the rhythm of their mothers' heartbeats. After birth, babies are comforted by music and song, especially when it mimics the sounds of the mother's body. What is more, an increasing catalogue of evidenced-based research has been produced that suggests music has a remarkably positive effect on patients experiencing a variety of medical conditions across the lifespan. For example, music has a demonstrably positive effect on management of mood, emotional and behavioral disorders; it has a rehabilitative effect on stroke patients; and it may have a therapeutic effect on patients with heart, respiratory, and blood-pressure disorders.[4]

Music thus may helpfully be employed as a tool to ease suffering, to create a meditative environment, and to soothe anxiety for sick and dying persons. Music also helps to reduce the impact of the beeping and buzzing sounds of medical equipment used in hospitals and care facilities. Of course, caregivers should be attentive to the reactions of their clients to music, mindful of volume, genre, and the regularity with which music is played. If music agitates or adds to distress, it should obviously be removed. With thoughtful application, however, music can be an intensely beneficial aid and comfort to persons negotiating pain and illness.

## Contemplative tools

Spiritual contemplation and meditative practices are found throughout the world's religious traditions. In each case, the contemplative attempts to enter into a focused state of mind or consciousness toward the aim of some spiritual gain. That gain may be defined in many ways: clarity of mind; enlightenment; mystical union with God; self-transcendence; tranquility; and so on. Meditative practice is called *practice* because it presupposes that a person will have to exercise deliberately his or her mental focus in order to achieve the desired state of consciousness and the spiritual benefits that flow from meditation.

While meditation pertains foremost to the focused mind, the mind cannot be focused without the discipline and control of the body. It is for this reason that meditation is often accompanied by physical gestures, postures, and activities. Physical gestures include such things as mudras (or ritual motions performed with one's hands) and the composition of facial expressions. Postures include manners of sitting, standing, and lying down in deliberate positioning of the body. Activities can include walking, bowing, dancing, and balancing.

Typically meditative activities are repetitive and sometimes practiced almost unceasingly by religious professionals (clergy, monks, nuns, and so on). For all people, contemplative practice can help in the processes of discerning right action; maintaining equanimity during adversity; and achieving control over thought and deed. For persons who are sick or dying, different forms of meditation (especially those drawn from within the dying person's own religious tradition or faith base) can especially help reduce pain; clarify the mind; induce a sense of peace; elicit spiritual wisdom; and prepare one for death and the encounter with what lies beyond. Meditative practices include:

1 *Prayer* is an essential component to contemplative practice. Prayer exists in many forms, with some forms being better situated to one context than others. Prayer can be personal and petitionary, where one brings either uttered or silently expressed requests and needs to God. Prayer can also be personal but wordless and without explicit content, whereby one seeks merely to empty the mind and enter into the presence of the Divine. Prayer may be personal and intercessory, where an individual prays on behalf of the needs of others. Prayer may also be communal. Communal prayer may occur in the formal settings of liturgical worship or in informal settings such as when staff pray together before a meeting or when people pray together online. Communal prayer may be petitionary, intercessory, and even silent, as when silence is observed in religiously plural settings or when a group of people silently meditates together as part of worship.

   In all of its forms, prayer can be a powerful complement to other practical aspects of caregiving. Help with prayer can be sought from clergy, chaplains, rabbis, imams, and so on. It is often useful and necessary to incorporate the aid of religious professionals in the art of care. Help for lay persons may be found in prayer books, such as Joan Guntzelman's *124 Prayers for Caregivers* (Winona, Minnesota: Saint Mary's Press, 1995) and Annetta Dellinger and Karen Boerger's *Blessings and Prayers for Caregivers* (Saint Louis: Concordia Publishing House, 2010).

2 *Breathwork* refers to the contemplative art of focused breathing. Used for centuries in T'ai Chi, Buddhist and Hindu meditation practice, breathwork can be used to elicit a desired state of consciousness; to reduce pain; and to promote harmony and balance between body and mind. Much as breathwork is commonly practiced by women in labor, breathwork may also be helpfully employed to ease pain and induce calm in clients, especially at the end of life. In fact, the same sorts of breathing aids that midwives bring to laboring women can be used with people transitioning from life to death. Some resources that help further explain the goal and practice of breathwork include James Beard's *Thirteen Breaths to Freedom: An Introduction to Breathwork* (San Diego, California: Sacred Systems, 2011) and Nancy Zi's *The Art of Breathing: 6 Simple Lessons to Improve Performance, Health, and Well-Being* (Glendale, California: Frog Books, 2000).

3 *Guided visualization* is the practice of achieving a focused or relaxed state of mind through the suggested imagery offered by a guide. Such a guide could be a person, such as a meditation instructor, or an audio recording. Guided visualization can help suffering persons achieve a sense of wellbeing, understanding, and peacefulness. Once a script is learned, an individual can independently use the visualization as a meditative tool. Resources for guided visualization include: Andrew E. Schwartz, *Guided Imagery for Groups* (Duluth, Minnesota: Versa Press, 1995); Martin L. Rossman, M.D., *Guided Imagery for Self-Healing: An Essential Resource for Anyone Seeking Wellness* (Tiburon, California: H. J. Kramer and Novato, California: New

World Library, 2000); Lisa Summer, *Guided Imagery and Music in the Institutional Setting* (St. Louis: MMB Music, Inc., 1998).

4 *Spiritual discernment* is the process of using focused meditation and prayer in the effort to try to discern or understand God's will in one's life. In the sixteenth century, Saint Ignatius Loyola (founder of the Society of Jesus) achieved his own spiritual epiphany by a disciplined approach to prayer, imaginative biblical contemplation, and focused meditation on a series of questions about his life in relationship to God. Out of his experiences, Ignatius produced one of the more famous treatises on discernment, the *Spiritual Exercises*, which is a manual for instructors on how to guide others in the processes of discerning God's will in their lives. Although by no means exclusive in the art of spiritual discernment, Ignatius's work reveals the positive outcomes of intentionally praying and meditating upon one's unique personal gifts and their meritorious use for the good of others and therefore for God. Spiritual discernment today may be undertaken in a formal way with a director, in a retreat setting, or in private for those serious about engaging deeply in a life review. Helpful books on spiritual discernment practices include: Andy Alexander, S.J., Maureen McCann Waldron, and Larry Gillick, S.J., *Retreat in the Real World: Finding Intimacy with God Wherever You Are* (Chicago: Loyola Press, 2009); and Priscilla Shirer, *Discerning the Voice of God: How to Recognize When God Speaks* (Chicago: Moody Publishers, 2007).

## Film resources

An excellent way to enhance discussion about suffering, spirituality, dying, and bereavement is to use films and audiovisuals. There are hundreds of films that educators and caregivers could choose from to enliven conversation and bring illustrative examples of the human struggle with suffering into the classroom or workshop.[5] I have found it helpful to query my classrooms for suggestions about films they have seen or would like to use and discuss as a large group. If it is possible to allow for participants to contribute in this way, conversation will be more organic insofar as the material viewed reflects the voice of the group and the educational use of films correlatively will be even more impactful. Some film titles that my students have suggested and which have been successfully used in recent courses include the following, for which I have provided short synopses:

1 *The Messenger* (2009, Oscilloscope Films), directed by Oren Moverman. *The Messenger* tells the story of Will, a soldier injured in the Iraq War. After his injury, Will is reassigned to the "Casualty Notification Office," the division that informs families that their loved ones have been slain in battle. Will struggles to make sense of his own post-war life and relationships, even as his assignments uncomfortably bring him into the intimate grief spaces of families besieged with shattering loss.

2 *Melancholia* (2011, Magnolia Pictures), directed by Lars von Trier. *Melancholia* follows sisters Justine and Claire during the last days of life before Earth is destroyed in a collision with a rogue planet. Justine abandons hope early on, goes wild with grief, and sinks into a debilitating depression. Ultimately, Justine rises from her depression with acceptance of the inevitable, and offers her best comfort to Claire's young son before the end. Taken as an allegory for clinical depression (and the desperate fear that one may never be well) or literally as a science-fiction story, director Lars von Trier explores the unique effects of hopelessness in their varied forms.
3 *What Dreams May Come* (1998, Polygram), directed by Vincent Ward. In this film adaptation of Richard Matheson's novel by the same name, Chris and Annie struggle to hold their marriage together after the devastating deaths of their young son and daughter. Upon being killed in a car accident, Chris reunites with his children and waits in Paradise for his wife to live the rest of her mortal days. However, the pain of losing her family was more than Annie could bear, and she is condemned to Hell after taking her own life. At the risk of his own soul, Chris ventures into Hell to pull his grief-stricken wife back into grace through confrontation of their sorrow.
4 *The Fountain* (2006, 20th Century Fox, Regency Enterprises, Warner Bros.), directed by Darren Aronofsky. In this highly abstract film, the stories of a Spanish explorer, a present-day medical researcher, and a future space-traveler cross over as each searches for the means to escape death. With its stunning imagery and beautiful tonalities, *The Fountain* plays as an elegy on mortality, fear of loss, grief, letting go, the inevitably of death, and the unfathomable potential for transcendence. The film highlights the interconnectedness of all living things through our shared experience of death and the emergence of new life in its wake.
5 *My Sister's Keeper* (2009, New Line Cinema), directed by Nick Cassavetes. After learning that she was conceived solely as a perfect donor-match for her ailing older sister, eleven-year-old Anna seeks medical emancipation from her parents to prevent them from taking one of her kidneys. Anna must confront her feelings of betrayal by her parents even as their marriage strains with the weight of their ethical burden and the sorrow of their older daughter's descent towards death.
6 *The Bucket List* (2007, Warner Bros. Pictures), directed by Rob Reiner. In this charming tale, two cancer patients from different backgrounds escape from their hospital ward and travel the world as they rush to experience all the things they hoped to do before they die. As they bond during their journey of discovery, they forge a deep friendship while clinging to life at the brink of death.

## Book resources

Book resources on the theology of suffering can be divided into primary and secondary source material. In this context, I am using the term "primary" to refer to critical and classic treatments of suffering and dying that often surface in the literature due to their enduring power to speak to an audience from generation to generation. I here also use this term to refer to contemporary works that have been popularly well received and widely disseminated. There are, of course, countless works of fiction, non-fiction, and poetry found throughout world literature that examine human suffering, so I am only here selecting some of the more accessible works I use effectively in the classroom. The secondary resources I here reference represent a selection of scholarly and clinical resources that provide a depth and range of research topics that exceeded the scope of this book. Each of the primary and secondary sources here referenced will prove assets to further study of suffering and dying.

### *Primary sources*

1 *The Book of Job. The Book of Job* is one of the world's oldest and foremost theological studies of the experience of pain. While one of the books of the Hebrew Bible, *Job* nevertheless stands on its own as among the greatest literary achievements of all time. The book relates the story of the righteous and prosperous man, Job, who prays and worships faithfully in thanksgiving to God for all his blessings. Job's faith, however, is tested when God permits Satan (literally, the *Adversary*) to destroy first Job's household (taking everything, including the lives of his children) and then Job's health. For, Satan has raised the question: will Job continue to be faithful to God when he has nothing? The Adversary contends, it is easy to give praise when all is well, but in times of hardship, does not trust in God fail? A poetic dialogue ensues between Job and four friends, who varyingly attempt to console and rebuke Job for some presumed sin. The dialogue itself raises questions about whether anyone is righteous, about the therapeutic character of suffering, and the forgiveness of God for those who repent. In a dramatic turn in the narrative, God himself emerges to reframe Job's experience of suffering against the backdrop of God's unsearchable and fathomless power over creation. The dialogue concludes with Job's repentance before God and the restoration of his household and the birth of new children. The narrative retains an ambiguous quality though; for in the end, God has still allowed the death of Job's first children, who cannot themselves be restored. There is no satisfying answer to this fact. Stephen Mitchell's *The Book of Job* (New York: HarperPerennial, 1992) is a fine translation of this biblical text, complete with a scholarly introduction. In addition, several good applications of the book to modern-day questions may help broaden the reader's interpretation of the text. Two include Ellen van Wolde's *Job's God* (London: SCM Press, 2004) and Joseph Kelly's *The Problem of Evil in the Western Tradition: From the Book of Job to Modern Genetics* (Collegeville: Liturgical Press, 2002).
2 C. S. Lewis' *The Problem of Pain* (New York: Harper One, 2001) and *A Grief Observed* (New York: Harper One, 2001). Originally published

in 1940 and 1961 respectively, these books represent the philosophical and personal range of Lewis' investigation into the problem of human suffering. In the earlier treatise, Lewis responds to the philosophical problem of suffering by: 1) clarifying and redefining what is meant by God's goodness and God's power; and 2) arguing that humans need pain as a therapeutic remedy to moral and spiritual corruption. He concludes, in short, that suffering restores people to a humble awareness and dependence upon God. In the second book, published two decades later, Lewis writes about his own experience of grief after the death of his wife. The book studies the effect of grief on the body and mind, openly admitting that religion can add to grief when and if it purports simple platitudes or superficial consolations. For, in the face of personal loss, an almighty deity can seem more enemy than friend for allowing such hardships to be dealt. Lewis' work reflects on the grief process, as he experiences it. Even though his grief is not overcome, through bearing witness to his own processes Lewis comes to a restored trust in God's constructive use of suffering.

3 Viktor Frankl's *Man's Search For Meaning* (Boston: Beacon Press, 2006). Frankl's book, published first in Austria in 1946, is a gripping tale of life in the Nazi concentration camps. As a psychologist, Frankl brought his clinical observations to life in the camps, as he contemplated the psychological impact of the experience on prisoners. Frankl surveys three key psychological states that prisoners endured: 1) shock at the onset of the experience as one's established sense of life, purpose, and personal meaning were radically interrupted; 2) apathy to the horror and death that abounded, which was a necessary yet psychologically risky coping mechanism for prisoners; and 3) the challenge of acclimating to life outside the camps for those who survived. The final stage, namely freedom, produced profound difficulties for the survivors, who found themselves irrevocably transformed and thus deeply altered in relationship to their former sense of self, occupations, homes, other people, and so on. Frankl contends that in the experience of incalculable suffering, people can still find hope and, moreover, can grow spiritually as they discover the saving graces of love and faith. Without faith, Frankl offers that prisoners perished; with it, they could endure. Frankl's text is one of the most well-read documents on the Holocaust. Its timeless appeal lies perhaps most in its eloquent witness to the transcendent power of love and love's ultimately liberating effect on the human spirit.

4 Harold Kushner's *When Bad Things Happen To Good People* (New York: Schocken Books, 1981). Rabbi Kushner's book[6] is a remarkable treatise on theodicy, born out of his own grappling with the question when his fourteen-year-old son died from the aging disease progeria. This devastating experience transformed Kushner's understanding of suffering and illuminated Kushner's sense of helpful and unhelpful ways of responding to loss. Recognizing that some degree of unjust suffering is the common lot of

humanity, Kushner does not ask *why* bad things happen to good people but rather *when*. For, when bad things happen, Kushner asserts that people often are at a loss how to help those they care about. Well-wishers say things such as, "God does not put on people more than they can carry" or "God must have had a good reason for X." Such ideas, however, elicit in the suffering person a sense of personal accountability for the thing that happened ("If I were weaker, God would not have burdened me so greatly") as well as confusing ideas about God's power and goodness. (It is obviously evil when a regular person kills someone; but if God wills or allows a murder, then it must inexplicably be somehow good.) Kushner holds that these ideas are human efforts to justify God and/or efforts to safeguard ourselves by means of blaming the victim. If a tragedy can somehow be causally linked to the person afflicted, then the rest of us can feel protected from tragedy insofar as we see ourselves as better behaved and so on. If God is at once all-good and all-powerful, no matter what horrible things have happened, then the universe can be seen as safe and just. Kushner holds, to the contrary, that God does not control all life in a micro-managerial fashion and nor is the universe unquestionably fair or safe. People are vulnerable, and suffering will occur. The thing that matters most in suffering is not why it happens but how people respond, especially when they do so with resiliency, compassion, and hope. It is in and through human kindness and empathy that Kushner sees God most present in suffering. While God's power is somewhat impugned in Kushner's model, he holds that a more honest and compassionate human response to suffering emerges in light of a more wholesome conception of God's inability either to cause or to stop it.

5 Mitch Albom's *Tuesdays With Morrie* (New York: Random House, 1997). This famous book chronicles the conversations between Mitch Albom and his college sociology professor, Morrie Schwartz. When Albom learned that his former teacher was dying of Lou Gehrig's disease, Albom began weekly visits on Tuesdays to spend time with his friend. The wisdom garnered in those visits comprises the basis of the book as Morrie and Mitch discuss the world, self-pity, family, emotions, fear of aging, money, life ongoing, marriage, culture, forgiveness, and inevitable death. As their time wanes thin, Albom gains tremendous insight into living well, relating well, and ultimately into dying well. Morrie also published his own insights into living with disability and enduring a terminal illness in his work *Letting Go: Morrie's Reflections on Living While Dying* (New York: Walker & Co., 1996). A helpful complement to both these texts is a three-part series of interviews between Morrie Schwartz and Ted Koppel, produced for Nightline, now available in DVD as *ABC News presents Morrie Schwartz – Lessons on Living* (2005). Together, these works provide a powerful, personal witness to courage in the face of death, the potential of illness to bring about a final stage of personal growth, and the spiritual illumination to which suffering may give rise.

***Secondary sources***

1 *Baywood Publishing Company titles*. The Baywood Publishing Company in Amityville, New York, specializes in scholarly and professional publications in the humanities and social sciences. Among their key content areas is a broad corpus of research and practitioner-based texts on death and bereavement. I have found their catalogue in its breadth to be a truly invaluable resource in all aspects of the study of suffering, dying, and related spiritual issues. Among the most useful resources for classroom use are their edited volumes in the *Death, Value, and Meaning Series*, now under the editorship of Dr Dale Lund.
2 *Spirited Practices: Spirituality and the Helping Professions*, edited by Fran Gale, Natalie Bolzan, and Dorothy McRae-McMahon (Crows Nest: Australia, 2007). This collection of articles examines the interconnections and challenges of professional practice and spiritual openness for those in caregiving professions. Aware that today's helping professionals need enhanced dexterity in understanding and responding to the spectrum of spiritual needs of clients, this volume seeks to enhance the skill set of professionals across the disciplines of social work, psychology, education, healthcare, and ministry.
3 Charles Topper's *Spirituality in Pastoral Counseling and the Community Helping Professions* (New York: The Haworth Press, 2003). This book is a practical tool for helping professionals. It comes equipped with a range of resources to guide caregivers in both the theory and practice of incorporating spiritual care within their professional disciplines. Topper provides tools for doing spiritual assessments, for processing the spiritual care needs of clients, and for incorporating spiritual caregiving praxis within professional organizations and management structures. Of particular merit, Topper provides a chapter on clinical assessment of spiritual needs, complete with examples of interview and survey tools, as well as instructions for building one's own instruments.
4 Richard F. Groves and Henriette Anne Klauser's *The American Book of Living and Dying: Lessons in Healing Spiritual Pain* (Berkeley and Toronto: Celestial Arts, 2009).[7] This book, oft referenced in this current text, is a delightfully accessible and engaging resource. The book presents a history of spiritual care for the dying, case studies, and a resource chapter. In particular, the case studies presented are tenderly written, insightful, and truly enriching. They present accounts of varied aspects of spiritual pain and illustrate for the caregiver profound lessons about hope in the face of terminal illness.
5 Trudy Harris' *Glimpses of Heaven: True Stories of Hope & Peace at the End of Life's Journey* (Grand Rapids, Michigan: Revell, 2008). This final resource is a beautiful collection of the stories of forty-four terminal patients in a hospice context. Harris listens closely to the wisdom each individual has to share about life and death from the perspective that

counts, namely, the perspective of the dying. These sorts of lessons are perhaps the most useful in any consideration of suffering and dying because they come from firsthand experience. Through her subjects, Harris allows the thoughts and visions of the dying to shed light on the meaning and experience of death in a courageous and attentive way.

## Conclusion

At the conclusion of this discussion on tools for thinking about suffering, and indeed at the conclusion of this book, I would like to recall an observation made in the opening chapter: nothing engages the theological imagination more than the experience of human pain and suffering. Pain, suffering, and the inevitability of death demarcate the limits of human, mortal existence. Yet, somewhat ironically, they also invite people into the deepest experiences of faith, hope, and the promise that life fundamentally transcends those limits. Pain and suffering also elicit opportunities for unparalleled expressions of compassionate care between people as we meet and tend to one another in loving address of our common needs and shared frailties.

It is a blessing that people meet each other at different points in their journeys, so that some are well, while others are declining. In this way, it becomes possible for essentially frail and limited people to act, for a time, out of their strength in service to others. The great reward for those who are so daring as to meet the challenge of caring for others is that they have unmatched opportunities to gain wisdom in advance of their own years and experience. This wisdom can become the foremost guide to living well, making good choices, building strong relationships, and valuing each moment as the treasure that it is. I would like to conclude with a telling anecdote recalled in Trudy Harris' book mentioned above. Here Harris captures the essence of what dying can do for the living:

> A patient who was afraid to die lying flat on his back asked me to hold him in a sitting position as he was dying. Moments before he died he said to me, "Trudy, there is no such thing as time. Dying is like walking from the living room into the dining room, there are no beginnings or endings." The words he spoke were in response to my looking at my watch as I foolishly counted his respirations, and he smiled a very patient smile as he said it. Then he closed his eyes and died. There are so many new insights, so many opportunities to think and understand in a whole new way when seeing from the perspective of the patient who is moments away from entering heaven. There are so many lessons people are trying to teach us moments before they die. We had better listen. We are standing on holy ground during these moments, and we dare not miss one of them.[8]

# Notes

## 1 Theodicy and the question: how can God allow pain?

1 The synoptic Gospels record his words from the Cross: "My God, my God, why have you forsaken me?"
2 Karl Rahner, *Foundations of Christian Faith* (New York: The Crossroad Publishing Company, 1978), p. 34.
3 For an interesting article on the proper interpretation of absolute dependency in Schleiermacher's description of the Christian state of mind, see George Behrens, "Feeling of absolute dependence or absolute feeling of dependence? (What Schleiermacher really said and why it matters)," *Religious Studies* Vol. 34, No. 4 (December 1998): 471–81.
4 Jon Sobrino, "Theology in a suffering world," in *Pluralism and Oppression*, edited by Paul F. Knitter (Lanham, Maryland: University Press of America, 1991).
5 All scripture quotes are from the New American Bible.
6 A good treatment of this pattern of thought is explored in Jack Nelson Pallmeyer's text *Is Religion Killing Us?* (Harrisburg, Pennsylvania: Trinity Press International, 2003). Here, Pallmeyer explores in comparative perspective Jewish, Christian, and Islamic explanations of corporate punishment and justifications for violence.
7 For example, HIV/AIDS has been famously interpreted as God's punishment for homosexuality and social liberalism.
8 End-time thinking can be found across the range of religious traditions. For a comparative discussion, consult Charles Kimball's *When Religion Becomes Evil* (New York: HarperOne, 2008).
9 Genesis 1:27–31.
10 Genesis 3:16–19.
11 Romans 6:23.
12 C. S. Lewis, *The Problem of Pain* (San Francisco: HarperSanFrancisco, 2001). Original publication was in 1940.
13 Lewis, p. 86.
14 See, for example, Catherine Keller's *Apocalypse Now and Then* (Boston: Beacon Press, 1993); Rosemary Radford Ruether's *Gaia and God* (San Francisco: HarperSanFrancisco, 1992); and Sallie McFague's *The Body of God* (Minneapolis: Fortress Press, 1993).
15 The question of how Jesus' death is salvific is the central question of Christian theology across its two-thousand-year history. Discussion of the history of this theology will take place in Chapters Four and Five.
16 Dorothee Soelle, *Suffering* (Philadelphia: Fortress Press, 1984).
17 Douglas John Hall, *God and Human Suffering: An Exercise in the Theology of the Cross* (Minneapolis: Augsburg Publishing House, 1986).

18 Hall, p. 132.
19 From the English translation of Henri-Jérôme Gagey's plenary address "De la Résurrection du Seigneur. Y a-t-il un sens à parler d'un événement historique accessible à la foi seule?" presented at the Leuven Encounters in Systematic Theology VIII conference in Leuven, Belgium on 28 October 2011.
20 Louis J. Puhl, S.J., *The Spiritual Exercises of St. Ignatius: Based on Studies in the Language of the Autograph* (Chicago: Loyola Press, 1951), p. 151.
21 Research in the relationship between disease, pain management, and psycho-social, relational, and spiritual stress factors has been well-synthesized and integrated for caregiver education in the Abundant Life Education Program, developed by Catholic Community Connection. Educator resources may be found at http://abundantlifecare.com.

**3 Suffering in the Bible, Part II**

1 See James W. Ermatinger, *Daily Life of Christians in Ancient Rome* (Westport, Connecticut: Greenwood, 2007). For an index of primary sources, see Dana Carleton Munro and Edith Bramhall, Eds, *The Early Christian Persecutions* (New York: Longman, Green, & Co., 1902).
2 For a helpful introduction, see Charles Puskas and David Crump, *An Introduction to the Gospels and Acts* (Grand Rapids, Michigan: William B. Eerdmans Publishing Company, 2008). Also see Stephen L. Harris, *The New Testament: A Student's Introduction* (New York; McGraw-Hill, 2012).
3 A helpful discussion of gospel portraits may be found in Bart D. Ehrman's *A Brief Introduction to the New Testament* (New York: Oxford University Press, 2004).
4 See Paul Foster, *The Apocryphal Gospels: A Very Short Introduction* (Oxford University Press, 2009).
5 See I. Howard Marshall, Stephen Travis, and Ian Paul, *Exploring the New Testament: A Guide to the Letters and Revelation*, Second Edition (Downers Grove, Illinois: InterVarsity Press, 2011).
6 See Brian Jones, *The Emperor Domitian* (New York and London: Routledge, 1992).
7 See Pheme Perkins, *The Book of Revelation* (Collegeville, Minnesota: Liturgical Press, 1983).

**4 Soteriology, Part I**

1 Gerard S. Sloyan, *Why Jesus Died* (Minneapolis: Fortress Press, 2004), p. 95.
2 This perspective on the historical Jesus and the first Christians is illustrated in Bart Ehrman's *Jesus: Apocalyptic Prophet of the New Millennium* (New York: Oxford University Press, 2001).
3 See Joel B. Green and Mark D. Baker, *Recovering the Scandal of the Cross: Atonement in New Testament and Contemporary Contexts* (Downers Grove, Illinois: IVP, 2000).
4 This understanding of New Testament soteriology recognizes that Christian claims about the Hebrew texts emerged in polemical fashion against traditional Jewish interpretations, causing tension between first-century Christian Jews and non-Christian Jews. Rosemary Radford Ruether's book *Faith and Fratricide: The Theological Roots of Anti-Semitism* (Eugene, OR: Wipf & Stock Publishers, 1996) fully establishes this claim. While the point here is not to focus on the roots of anti-Semitism in early Christianity, I think Ruether's model is particularly useful for showing how the Christians developed a model of salvation out of the Hebrew material. Other helpful texts that look at New Testament soteriology include: Michael Gorman, *Inhabiting the Cruciform God: Kenosis, Justification, and Theosis in Paul's Narrative Soteriology* (Grand Rapids, MI: Wm. B. Eerdmans Publishing Co., 2009); Ernest Best, *The*

*Temptation and the Passion: The Markan Soteriology* (Cambridge: Cambridge University Press, 1965); Simon J. Gathercole, *Where is Boasting: Early Jewish Soteriology and Paul's Response in Romans 1–5* (Grand Rapids, MI: Wm. B. Eerdmans Publishing Co., 2002).

5 Eusebius of Caesarea's *Ecclesiastical History* (Book X, Chapter 5) records the edict in which Constantine ends religious persecution of Christians.

6 See Gerald O'Collins, S.J., *Christology: A Biblical, Historical, and Systematic Study of Jesus* (New York: Oxford University Press, 1995).

7 This all came to a head when the fourth-century presbyter Arius began to preach that the Son was a unique creature whose existence was willed by the Father (borrowing from the language of Proverbs 8:23). Arius argued that the Son was not co-eternal with the Father. Arius' somewhat popular theory created a heated debate that lasted from 318 to 325, when Constantine convened the Council of Nicaea, at which time the language of *homo-ousios* (or same substance) was employed to express the consubstantiality of the Father with the Son. This language was adopted into the Creed of Nicaea in 325 and was again ratified at the First Council of Constantinople in 381, along with the articulation that Jesus had a truly human soul (not just human flesh). The patristic theologian Athanasius was particularly ferocious in confirming the faith of Nicaea and is largely responsible for defining a theology of the Incarnation. In his work *On the Incarnation*, Athanasius drives home the point that if the Son had not truly become man – in all aspects of the human person including the soul – then the whole human person would not have been saved by His work. The later councils of the era, such as Ephesus in 431 and Chalcedon in 451, were keen to highlight this same point. They concluded time and again that Jesus must be truly human in all aspects (body, nature, and volition), as well as truly God, if his death is to have saving merit for humanity. By the fifth century, when Augustine takes up his masterwork *De Trinitate*, the language of one substance, three hypostases is taken for granted. He turns to an exploration of the inner life of the Trinity, where he argues that the threeness of God is rooted in the relations of begetting, begotten, and proceeding.

8 Walter H. Principe, C.S.B., *Introduction to Patristic and Medieval Theology* (Toronto: Pontifical Institute of Medieval Studies, 1982, 1992).

9 J. Patut Burns, S.J., "The concept of satisfaction in medieval redemption theory," *Theological Studies*, Vol. 36, No. 2 (June 1975): 285–304. Also, see primary source readings in John R. Sheetes, S.J., Ed., *The Theology of the Atonement: Readings in Soteriology* (Englewood Cliffs, New Jersey: Prentice Hall, 1967).

10 In other words, the weight of the sin was determined on the basis of the one who was offended. In the feudal system, if a peasant injured another peasant the offence was considered less than if that same injury was done by a peasant against the lord of the manor.

11 See Peter Matheson's *Reformation Christianity* (Minneapolis: Fortress Press, 2007).

12 Consult Richard Marius's *Martin Luther: The Christian Between God and Death* (Cambridge, MA: Belknap Press of Harvard University Press, 1999).

13 For an introduction to John Calvin and Reformed theology, see Michael A. Mullett's *John Calvin* (London: Routledge, 2011).

14 For a survey of the origins of the Church of England, see Ethan Shagan's *Rule of Moderation* (Cambridge; New York: Cambridge University Press, 2011).

15 For a concise collection of Luther's writings, see John Dillenberger, Ed., *Martin Luther, Selections From His Writings* (New York: Doubleday, 1962).

16 See Alister McGrath's discussion in *Historical Theology: An Introduction to the History of Christian Thought* (Malden, MA: Blackwell Publishers, 1998), pp. 185–86.

17 Quoted in John R. Sheetes, S.J., Ed., *The Theology of the Atonement: Readings in Soteriology* (Englewood Cliffs, New Jersey: Prentice Hall, 1967), p. 27.

18 Paul Althaus, *The Theology of Martin Luther* (Philadelphia: Fortress Press, 1966), pp. 205–6.
19 John Calvin, *The Institutes of Christian Religion*, edited by Tony Lane and Hilary Osborne (Grand Rapids: Baker Book House, 1999), pp. 132–33.
20 David Wright, "The atonement in Reformation theology," *European Journal of Theology*, Vol. 8 No. 1 (1999): 37–48.
21 For a fuller discussion of Trent on these questions, see McGrath's treatment in *Historical Theology*, pp. 190–95.

**5 Soteriology, Part II**

1 Dorothee Soelle, *Suffering* (Philadelphia: Fortress Press, 1975), pp. 134–35.
2 Alister McGrath, *Historical Theology* (Oxford: Blackwell Publishers, 1998).
3 For the classic work in this area, see Albert Schweitzer's (1875–1965) *Quest for the Historical Jesus*, translated by W. Montgomery (Mineola, New York: Dover Publications, 2005), originally published in 1911 by Adam and Charles Black, London.
4 See James K. Beilby and Paul R. Eddy, Eds, *The Historical Jesus: Five Views* (Grove City, Illinois: IVP Academic, 2009).
5 The following descriptive terms, generally referenced here, are derived from Neil Ormerod's *Introducing Contemporary Theologies: The What and the Who of Theology Today* (Maryknoll, New York: Orbis, 1997): historical-critical; hermeneutical; suspicious of authority; pluralistic; anti-metaphysical; scriptural; personalist; dialectical; and seeking foundations.
6 David Miller, *A Century of War: The History of Worldwide Conflict in the 20th Century* (New York: Crescent Books, 1997).
7 Ibid., p. 7.
8 Ibid., p. 21.
9 Ibid., p. 45.
10 "The worst genocides of the 20th century," www.scaruffi.com/politics/dictat.html
11 Terry Stafford, *Deadly Dictators: Masterminds of 20th Century Genocide* (CreateSpace, 2010), p. 35.
12 Catherine Keller, *Apocalypse Now and Then* (Minneapolis, Minnesota: Fortress Press, 1996).
13 Dorothee Soelle, *Suffering* (Philadelphia: Fortress Press, 1975), p. 32.
14 Ibid., p. 148.
15 Ibid., p. 150.
16 Jon Sobrino, "Theology in a suffering world," in *Pluralism and Oppression: Theology in World Perspective*, edited by Paul F. Knitter (Lanham, Maryland: University of America Press, 1991).
17 There are many fine feminist treatments of women in the Christian biblical and theological traditions. A good, introductory survey is to be found in Rosemary Radford Ruether's *Women and Redemption: A Theological History* (Minneapolis: Fortress Press, 1998).
18 "Womanism" describes African-American feminist theological and philosophical projects.
19 Delores Williams, *Sisters in the Wilderness* (Maryknoll, New York: Orbis, 1995).
20 In Hebrew custom, which was tolerant of plural marriage and multiple sexual partners for men, barren wives could legally obtain an heir through the surrogate womb of a handmaid.
21 Hispanic or Latina feminist theologies.
22 Sallie McFague, *The Body of God* (Minneapolis: Augsburg Fortress Press, 1993), pp. 107–12.

**6 Death in comparative perspective**

1 Elisabeth Kubler-Ross, Ed., *Death: The Final Stage of Growth* (New York: Simon & Schuster, 1975), p. 167.
2 See Rabbi Earl A. Grollman, "Death in Jewish thought," in *Death and Spirituality*, edited by Kenneth Doka and John D. Morgan (Amityville, New York: Baywood Publishers, 1993), pp. 26–27.
3 Kenneth Kramer, "Hebraic attitudes toward death," in Kramer's *The Sacred Art of Dying* (Mahwah, New York: Paulist Press, 1988), p. 123.
4 Grollman, "Death in Jewish thought," pp. 23–25.
5 Ibid., p. 28.
6 The Hadith are the written traditions about Muhammad and his companions that serve as a complementary text to the revelation in the Qu'ran.
7 Kramer, p. 160.
8 Jane Idelman Smith and Yvonne Yazbeck Haddad, *The Islamic Understanding of Death and Resurrection* (New York: Oxford University Press, 2002), p. 31.
9 Ibid., p. 34.
10 See Kramer, pp. 164–66.
11 Ibid., p. 32.
12 Jaroslav Havelka, "The problem of death and dying in major Eastern traditions," in *Readings in Thanatology*, edited by John D. Morgan (Amityville, New York: Baywood Publishing, 1997), p. 506.
13 Francesca Fremantle and Chogyam Trungpa, trans., *The Tibetan Book of the Dead* (Boston and London: Shambhala, 1987), pp. 93–94.
14 Kramer, p. 87.

**7 Issues in spiritual caregiving for the suffering and dying**

1 David Weiss Halivni, *Breaking the Tablets: Jewish Theology After the Shoah*, edited by Peter Ochs (Lanham, MD: Rowman & Littlefield Publishers, Inc., 2007), p. 16.
2 Viktor Frankl, *Man's Search for Meaning* (New York: Pocket Books, 1984), pp. 98–99.
3 Joan Halifax, *Being with Dying: Cultivating Compassion and Fearlessness in the Presence of Death* (Boston: Shambhala, 2009), pp. 179–80.
4 Cathy Siebold, *The Hospice Movement: Easing Death's Pains* (New York; Toronto: Maxwell Macmillan International, 1992).
5 Dame Cicely Saunders, *Living with Dying: A Guide to Palliative Care* (Oxford and New York: Oxford University Press, 1995).
6 Elisabeth Kübler-Ross, *On Death and Dying* (New York: Macmillan, 1969).
7 Patrice O'Connor, "A clinical paradigm for exploring spiritual concerns," in *Death and Spirituality*, edited by Kenneth J. Doka and John D. Morgan (Amityville, New York: Baywood Publishing, 1993), pp. 133–42.
8 Richard Groves and Henriette Anne Klausen, *The American Book of Dying: Lessons in Healing Spiritual Pain* (Berkeley, California: Celestial Arts, 2005).
9 Ibid., pp. 35–36.
10 Halifax, p. 202.
11 Maggie Callanan and Patricia Kelley, *Final Gifts: Understanding the Special Awareness, Needs, and Communications of the Dying* (New York: Bantam Books, 1997), p. 2.
12 Please see the full explanation of the FICA tool on the GWish webpage at www.gwumc.edu/gwish/clinical/fica.cfm
13 David K. Meagher and Craig P. Bell, "Perspectives on death in the African American community," in *Death and Spirituality*, edited by Kenneth Doka and John Morgan (Amityville, New York: Baywood Publishing, 1993), pp. 122–23.

14 Ibid., p. 125.
15 See the United Nations Population Fund data at www.unfpa.org/gender/violence.htm
16 For example, the twentieth-century genocides in the Former Yugoslavia and Rwanda.
17 To learn more, see the United Nations Inter-Agency Project on Human Trafficking at www.no-trafficking.org
18 Some excellent works to consult here include Mary Daly, *Gyn/Ecology* (Boston: Beacon Press, 1978); Marcella Althaus Reid, *From Feminist to Indecent Theology* (London: SCP, 2011); Ada Maria Isasi Diaz, *En La Lucha: A Hispanic Women's Liberation Theology* (Minneapolis: Fortress Press, 1993); and Emilie M. Townes, Ed., *Troubling in My Soul: Womanist Perspectives on Evil and Suffering* (Maryknoll, New York: Orbis Books, 1993).
19 David Kessler, *The Rights of the Dying: A Companion for Life's Final Moments* (New York: HarperCollins Publishers, 1997).
20 C. Murray Parkes, "Bereavement: What most people should know," in *Readings in Thanatology*, edited by John D. Morgan (Amityville, New York: Baywood Publishing, 1997), pp. 241–53.
21 Ibid., p. 241.
22 Kenneth J. Doka, "The spiritual crisis of bereavement," in *Death and Spirituality*, edited by Kenneth Doka and John Morgan (Amityville, New York: Baywood Publishing, 1993), p. 185.
23 Ibid., pp. 188–91.
24 Howard Raether, "Rituals, beliefs, and grief," in *Death and Spirituality*, edited by Kenneth Doka and John Morgan (Amityville, New York: Baywood Publishing, 1993), pp. 207–15.
25 C. S. Lewis, *The Problem of Pain* (New York: HarperSanFrancisco, 1996), p. xii.

## 8 A toolbox for dealing with suffering and death

1 Kristine A. Culp, *Vulnerability and Glory: A Theological Account* (Louisville, Kentucky: Westminster John Knox Press, 2010).
2 Kathleen Dowling Singh, Ph.D., "Taking A Spiritual Inventory" from www.pbs.org/wnet/onourownterms/articles/inventory.html.
3 This is a partial list of Dowling Singh's inventory questions, cited in full at www.pbs.org/wnet/onourownterms/articles/inventory.html. For a full presentation of Dowling Singh's work, see her book *The Grace in Dying: How We Are Transformed Spiritually as We Die* (San Francisco: HarperSanFrancisco, 1998).
4 For a broad-range bibliography on music therapy research and its effective applications, consult the American Music Therapy Association's medical research database at www.musictherapy.org.
5 There are abundant educational films about hospice, dying, euthanasia, bereavement, and so on. One very good series is Bill Moyer's *On Our Own Terms* (Princeton: Films for the Humanities and Sciences, 2000). An annotated discussion of such educational materials can be found in Richard Pacholski, "Spirituality and death in audiovisuals," in *Death and Spirituality*, edited by Kenneth J. Doka and John D. Morgan (Amityville: Baywood Publishing Company, 1993). I choose here to focus on popular movies, which reflect the broader conversation about death and dying in mainstream culture. I find a combination of both types of audiovisual materials to be most well-rounded and effective in the classroom.
6 Kushner also has a video lecture of this material in "When Bad Things Happen to Good People" (Advent Video, 1992).
7 This book was originally published by Celestial Arts under the title *The American Book of Dying*.
8 Trudy Harris, *Glimpses of Heaven: True Stories of Hope & Peace at the End of Life's Journey* (Grand Rapids, Michigan: Revell, 2008), p. 20.

# Index